LOW
FAT
COOKING

Edited by
Carol Bateman

Contents

This edition first published 1980 by
Octopus Books Limited
59 Grosvenor Street, London W1

Reprinted 1981

© 1980 Octopus Books Limited

ISBN 0 7064 1249 4

Produced by Mandarin Publishers Ltd
22a Westlands Road,
Quarry Bay, Hong Kong
Printed in Hong Kong

FRONTISPIECE: SLIMMER'S DELIGHT *(page 23)*
(Photograph: Mushroom Growers' Association)

Weights and Measures

All measurements in this book are given in Metric, Imperial and American.

Measurements in weight in the Imperial and American system are the same. Liquid measurements are different, and the following table shows the equivalents:

Liquid measurements

1 Imperial pint	20 fluid ounces
1 American pint	16 fluid ounces
1 American cup	8 fluid ounces

Level spoon measurements are used in all recipes.

Spoon measurements

1 tablespoon	15 ml
1 teaspoon	5 ml

When preparing the recipes in this book, only follow one set of measures – they are not interchangeable.

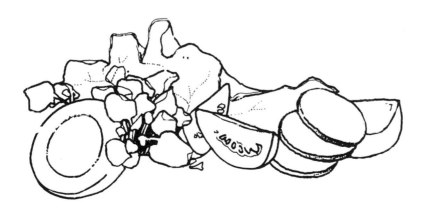

INTRODUCTION

Why a low fat cookbook? Because more and more people need, or wish, to restrict the amount of fat they eat, and require attractive and interesting low fat recipes to help them do so.

In this century there has been a dramatic rise in the incidence of arteriosclerotic disease in Western populations. Referred to in non-medical terms as 'hardening of the arteries', it can have fatal or crippling results. The increase in the numbers suffering from this disease has encouraged medical research – and diet, stress, smoking, obesity and environment have all been cited as possible causes. There is still much research to be done, but considerable medical evidence indicates that individuals at risk from development of arteriosclerosis should, at least, try to reduce their total fat intake. Many doctors and dieticians are now advising people who may have a family tendency to coronary heart disease, or other diseases related to arteriosclerosis, to adopt a diet relatively low in fat which will not lead to obesity.

As the recipes in this book show, it is quite easy to reduce the amount of fat eaten and still enjoy food. The question is, what kind of fat, and how much?

Over the past decades, the percentage of dietary energy from fat in Western diets has risen considerably – this is often measured as calories. The snacks and convenience foods of modern living tend to be high in fat. Much of this fat is what is known as 'saturated fat', and many doctors and dieticians consider that it is this saturated fat which must be reduced in the diet. Many suggest polyunsaturated fat as a replacement. So how do we know which is which?

Saturated fats
These are often of animal origin, and usually solid at room temperature. They are found in meat, milk, butter, cream, egg yolk, cheese, lard, suet and most ordinary margarines.

The prudent dieter should cut all fat from meat, and eat less meat, compensating with vegetables.

Milk should be skimmed, but dried skimmed milks which have had saturated vegetable fat added to them should be avoided.

Butter should be substituted with polyunsaturated margarine and cream with low fat natural (unflavored) yogurt.

Cheese varies in fat content – Cheshire and Lancashire are high in saturated fat; Edam, Gouda, and Camembert are slightly lower; curd cheese has about half the fat content of the full fat cheese, and cottage cheese has a very low fat content.

Polyunsaturated fats
Vegetable oils are particularly rich sources of polyunsaturated fats, which are generally liquid at room temperature. Different oils vary

8

in the amount of polyunsaturated fat they contain: safflower, sunflower and corn oils being particularly high and therefore most suitable.

When selecting margarine, check with the label that it is high in polyunsaturated fat.

Monounsaturated fats
Olive oil is particularly high in monounsaturated fat, which may be as suitable as polyunsaturated fat, but so far the evidence is inconclusive. Olive oil should therefore be used only in small amounts.

Cholesterol
Cholesterol is a form of fat, which occurs naturally in the human body. We need cholesterol for our normal digestive processes and cholesterol is made in the human liver for this purpose. However, very high levels of cholesterol in the blood may be a danger signal, particularly when there is a family history of coronary heart disease. If your doctor considers you should limit your cholesterol intake, bear in mind that foods with a high cholesterol content include: egg yolk, liver, brains, fish roes, chicken skin and some shell fish.

The recipes
Recipes in this book contain little *added* fat. Where fat has been used, it is vegetable oil or polyunsaturated margarine. The cook can decide which vegetable oil to select, taking into account the notes above. Foods high in cholesterol have been omitted, apart from the occasional egg yolk, so have meats with a particularly high fat content.

Cooking methods
Frying requires fat, so for low fat cooking use a non-stick frying pan and saucepan.
Cooking foil is another way to avoid using fat. Meat, fish, or vegetables, wrapped in foil, are delicious baked in their own juices.
Roasting bags (browning bags) also retain flavour and moisture in food, without the addition of fat. Fish, meat, vegetables and fruit can all be cooked in this way.
Boiling, baking and grilling (broiling) are all suitable methods of cooking for the low fat diet, provided extra fat is not added, particularly when grilling (broiling).

SOUPS

Lentil Soup

METRIC/IMPERIAL
1 ham knuckle
100 g/4 oz red lentils
100 g/4 oz split peas
1 large onion, peeled and roughly
  chopped
2 carrots, peeled and sliced
salt
freshly ground black pepper

AMERICAN
1 cured ham knuckle
½ cup red lentils
½ cup split peas
1 large onion, peeled and roughly
  chopped
2 carrots, peeled and sliced
salt
freshly ground black pepper

This soup has to be started the day before it is required.

Cover the ham knuckle with about 1.2 litres/2 pints/5 cups water, bring to boiling point and simmer for about 2 hours. Remove the ham knuckle and leave the liquid to cool overnight. Cover the lentils and split peas with water and leave to soak overnight.

Remove any fat from the surface of the ham stock (bouillon), and strain the liquid into a large, clean saucepan. Add the drained lentils and split peas, the onion and carrots. Bring to the boil and simmer for about 1 hour, or until all the vegetables are soft. Add salt and pepper towards the end of the cooking time.

Purée the soup in a blender, or press through a coarse sieve. If desired, the lean meat from the ham knuckle may be chopped and added to the soup after blending. Return to a clean saucepan and reheat before serving.

Serves 4 to 6
Total Calories: 660

Leek and Tomato Soup

METRIC/IMPERIAL
4 large leeks, finely chopped
4 large tomatoes, skinned and
  chopped
1 bay leaf
1 teaspoon mixed dried herbs
300 ml/½ pint water
300 ml/½ pint low fat natural
  yogurt
salt
freshly ground black pepper

AMERICAN
4 large leeks, finely chopped
4 large tomatoes, skinned and
  chopped
1 bay leaf
1 teaspoon mixed dried herbs
1¼ cups water
1¼ cups low fat unflavored yogurt
salt
freshly ground black pepper

Place the vegetables in a saucepan with the bay leaf and herbs. Add the water and simmer gently until the vegetables are soft. Remove the bay leaf and purée the soup in a blender or press through a coarse sieve. Return to the saucepan and stir in the yogurt and salt and pepper to taste. Heat through, without boiling, and serve immediately.
Serves 4
Total Calories: 240

Mushroom and Onion Broth

METRIC/IMPERIAL
450 g/1 lb onions, peeled and thinly
  sliced
1.75 litres/3 pints chicken stock
450 g/1 lb mushrooms, thinly sliced
4 teaspoons Dijon mustard
75 g/3 oz pasta shapes
salt
freshly ground black pepper
chopped fresh parsley to garnish

AMERICAN
1 lb onions, peeled and thinly sliced
7½ cups chicken bouillon
4 cups thinly sliced mushrooms
4 teaspoons Dijon mustard
¾ cup pasta shapes
salt
freshly ground black pepper
chopped fresh parsley to garnish

Put the onion in a large saucepan and add about half the chicken stock (bouillon). Bring to the boil and simmer for 15 to 20 minutes, or until the onions are soft. Add the mushrooms, the Dijon mustard and the remainder of the stock and bring to the boil again. Add the pasta shapes, salt and pepper; cover the pan and simmer gently for a further 10 to 15 minutes. Serve garnished with chopped parsley.
Serves 4
Total Calories: 470

Potato Cider Soup

METRIC/IMPERIAL

350 g/12 oz onions, peeled and
  sliced
450 g/1 lb cooking apples, peeled,
  cored and sliced
1 kg/2 lb potatoes, peeled and sliced
300 ml/½ pint cider
1.2 litres/2 pints beef stock (beef
  cubes may be used)
½ teaspoon mixed dried herbs
½ teaspoon ground coriander seed
150 ml/¼ pint low fat natural
  yogurt
salt
freshly ground black pepper
chopped chives or fresh mint to
  garnish

AMERICAN

¾ lb onions, peeled and sliced
1 lb baking apples, peeled, cored
  and sliced
2 lb potatoes, peeled and sliced
1¼ cups hard cider
5 cups beef bouillon (bouillon cubes
  may be used)
½ teaspoon mixed dried herbs
½ teaspoon ground coriander seed
⅔ cup low fat unflavored yogurt
salt
freshly ground black pepper
chopped chives or fresh mint to
  garnish

Put the onions, apples and potatoes in a saucepan and add the cider. Bring to the boil and cook briskly for 10 minutes, stirring from time to time. Add the stock (bouillon), dried herbs and coriander. Cover and simmer for about 1 hour, until all the vegetables are very tender.

Purée the soup in a blender or press through a coarse sieve. Return to the saucepan and stir in the yogurt, reserving 1 tablespoon for garnish. Season with salt and freshly ground pepper and reheat. Serve with a little yogurt swirled into each bowl and sprinkled with chopped chives or fresh mint.

Serves 5 to 6
Total Calories: 1240

POTATO CIDER SOUP, APPLE AND LENTIL SOUP *(page 14)*,
TURKEY CHESTNUT SOUP *(page 15)*,
CABBAGE AND APPLE SOUP *(page 18)*
(Photograph: Apple and Pear Development Council)

Apple and Lentil Soup

METRIC/IMPERIAL
*450 g/1 lb cooking apples, peeled,
  cored and chopped*
100 g/4 oz celery, chopped
2 large onions, peeled and chopped
*225 g/8 oz carrots, peeled and
  chopped*
225 g/8 oz red lentils
1-2 teaspoons curry powder
2 teaspoons tomato purée
1.75 litres/3 pints water or stock
salt
freshly ground black pepper

AMERICAN
*1 lb baking apples, peeled, cored
  and chopped*
1 cup chopped celery
2 large onions, peeled and chopped
½ lb carrots, peeled and chopped
1 cup red lentils
1-2 teaspoons curry powder
2 teaspoons tomato paste
7½ cups water or bouillon
salt
freshly ground black pepper

Put the chopped apples, celery, onions and carrots into a large saucepan. Wash and drain the lentils, then mix them with the vegetables. Add the curry powder and tomato purée (paste) and mix in well. Add the water or stock (bouillon) and season with salt and pepper. Bring slowly to the boil, cover and simmer gently for 1–1½ hours, until the lentils are soft.

Purée the soup in a blender, or press through a coarse sieve. Return the soup to the rinsed-out saucepan and reheat. Adjust the seasoning and serve.

Note: As a low-fat alternative to croûtons, serve cubes of wholemeal bread, about 1 cm/½ inch square, toasted until really brown and crisp.

Serves 5 to 6
Total Calories: 970

Turkey Chestnut Soup

METRIC/IMPERIAL
450 g/1 lb chestnuts
1.2 litres/2 pints turkey stock
½ teaspoon mixed dried herbs
2-3 sticks celery, chopped
75 g/3 oz onion, peeled and
  chopped
2 tablespoons cooking oil
450 g/1 lb apples, peeled, cored and
  sliced
salt
freshly ground black pepper
1-2 tablespoons lemon juice
150 ml/¼ pint low fat natural
  yogurt

AMERICAN
1 lb chestnuts
5 cups turkey bouillon
½ teaspoon mixed dried herbs
2-3 stalks celery, chopped
⅔ cup chopped onion
2 tablespoons cooking oil
1 lb apples, peeled, cored and sliced
salt
freshly ground black pepper
1-2 tablespoons lemon juice
⅔ cup low fat unflavored yogurt

Cut a cross through the shell on one side of each of the chestnuts and either boil them in water for 10 minutes or roast them in a hot oven until they split. Remove the outer shells and the inner brown skins. Put the chestnuts in a saucepan with the turkey stock (bouillon) and mixed herbs and simmer for about 20 minutes, until tender.

Fry the celery and onion in the oil until softened, then add the apples and cook gently until softened.

Purée the chestnuts and stock in a blender with the celery, onion and apples, then return the mixture to the rinsed-out saucepan. Add salt and pepper to taste and the lemon juice. Stir in the yogurt and reheat, but do not boil. If you like, serve garnished with pieces of crisply fried lean bacon.

Serves 5 to 6
Total Calories: 1450

Gazpacho

METRIC/IMPERIAL
¼ cucumber, peeled and finely
  chopped
450 g/1 lb tomatoes, skinned and
  chopped
½ red pepper, seeded and finely
  chopped
1 onion, peeled and finely chopped
2 tablespoons chopped fresh parsley
1 clove garlic, crushed
4 tablespoons olive oil or corn oil
3 tablespoons lemon juice
salt
freshly ground black pepper

AMERICAN
¼ cucumber, peeled and finely
  chopped
2 cups skinned and chopped
  tomatoes
½ red pepper, seeded and finely
  chopped
1 onion, peeled and finely chopped
2 tablespoons chopped fresh parsley
1 clove garlic, crushed
¼ cup olive oil or corn oil
3 tablespoons lemon juice
salt
freshly ground black pepper

Mix the finely chopped vegetables and parsley with the garlic, oil and lemon juice. Season with salt and pepper to taste and chill well before serving. If preferred, all the ingredients can be put into a blender and mixed until smooth. Serve cold with chunks of crusty bread.
Serves 4
Total Calories: 640

GAZPACHO
(Photograph: Mazola Pure Corn Oil)

Cabbage and Apple Soup

METRIC/IMPERIAL
2 tablespoons cooking oil
3 medium onions, peeled and sliced
750 g/1 ½ lb cooking apples,
  peeled, cored and sliced
½ large heart of Savoy cabbage,
  shredded and washed, or 450 g/
  1 lb spring greens, shredded and
  washed.
1.75 litres/3 pints well-flavoured
  stock
salt
freshly ground black pepper
2-3 tablespoons chopped fresh
  parsley

AMERICAN
2 tablespoons cooking oil
3 medium onions, peeled and sliced
1 ½ lb baking apples, peeled, cored
  and sliced
½ large heart Savoy cabbage,
  shredded and washed, or 1 lb fresh
  greens, shredded and washed
7 ½ cups well-flavored bouillon
salt
freshly ground black pepper
2-3 tablespoons chopped fresh
  parsley

Heat the oil in a frying pan (skillet) and fry the onions gently until soft and transparent. Stir in the apples and cabbage and continue cooking until the cabbage is bright green. Add the stock (bouillon), season with salt and pepper and simmer gently until the vegetables are soft, about 20 minutes.

Purée the soup in a blender or press through a coarse sieve. Add the chopped parsley, adjust the seasoning and reheat.

Serves 5 to 6
Total Calories: 740

Chilled Watercress and Yogurt Soup

METRIC/IMPERIAL
2 bunches watercress
225 g/8 oz potatoes, peeled and
* sliced*
1 onion, peeled and sliced
900 ml/1½ pints chicken stock
1 clove garlic, crushed
salt
freshly ground black pepper
150 ml/¼ pint low fat natural
* yogurt*

AMERICAN
2 bunches watercress
½ lb potatoes, peeled and sliced
1 onion, peeled and sliced
3¾ cups chicken bouillon
1 clove garlic, crushed
salt
freshly ground black pepper
⅔ cup low fat unflavored yogurt

Wash the watercress thoroughly in cold water and discard any tough stalks or yellow leaves. Set aside a few sprigs for garnish, and put the remainder of the watercress into a large saucepan with the potatoes, onion, stock (bouillon) and garlic. Season well with salt and pepper. Bring to the boil, then cover the pan and simmer until the potatoes and onion are quite soft.

Allow to cool, then purée the soup in a blender or rub through a coarse sieve. Taste and adjust the seasoning before stirring in the yogurt. Serve chilled, garnished with watercress sprigs.

Serves 4
Total Calories: 300

FIRST COURSES

One popular appetizer which has to be limited on a low fat diet is avocado pear. Any other fruit or fruit juice can be used for a refreshing start to a meal, as can most vegetables. However, care must be taken with any dressings used.

Some shellfish may have a high cholesterol content, so it is sensible to confine them to the occasional treat. Remember that all meat and some kinds of fish have a natural fat content, and, if chosen as a first course, will add considerably to the fat content of the meal.

Crab and Apple Cocktail

METRIC/IMPERIAL
2 medium crabs or 225 g/8 oz white
  crab meat
450 g/1 lb crisp apples
Sauce:
2 tablespoons wine vinegar
150 ml/¼ pint low fat natural
  yogurt
grated rind and juice of 1 orange
½ teaspoon French mustard
2 teaspoons Worcestershire sauce
salt
freshly ground black pepper
Garnish:
watercress sprigs
crab legs

AMERICAN
2 medium crabs or ½ lb white crab
  meat
1 lb crisp apples
Sauce:
2 tablespoons wine vinegar
⅔ cup low fat unflavored yogurt
grated rind and juice of 1 orange
½ teaspoon French mustard
2 teaspoons Worcestershire sauce
salt
freshly ground black pepper
Garnish:
watercress sprigs
crab legs

Pick the white meat from the crabs and flake it up. Peel, core and dice the apples, reserving half an apple unpeeled, for garnish.

For the sauce, combine the vinegar, yogurt, orange rind and juice, mustard and Worcestershire sauce. Season with salt and freshly ground black pepper. Mix together the sauce, crab meat and diced apple.

Arrange the mixture in scallop shells or individual ramekin dishes or glasses. Garnish with watercress sprigs, thin slices from the unpeeled apple and the crab legs, if available.
Serves 4
Total Calories: 620

CRAB AND APPLE COCKTAIL
(Photograph: Apple and Pear Development Council)

Ratatouille

<table>
<tr><td>METRIC/IMPERIAL</td><td>AMERICAN</td></tr>
<tr><td>450 g/1 lb button mushrooms</td><td>4 cups button mushrooms</td></tr>
<tr><td>1 medium aubergine</td><td>1 medium eggplant</td></tr>
<tr><td>2 tablespoons vegetable oil, or olive oil</td><td>2 tablespoons vegetable oil, or olive oil</td></tr>
<tr><td>4 medium tomatoes, skinned, quartered and seeded</td><td>4 medium tomatoes, skinned, quartered and seeded</td></tr>
<tr><td>1 small green pepper, seeded and quartered</td><td>1 small green pepper, seeded and quartered</td></tr>
<tr><td>225 g/8 oz courgettes, thickly sliced</td><td>1½ cups thickly sliced zucchini</td></tr>
<tr><td>1 clove garlic, crushed</td><td>1 clove garlic, crushed</td></tr>
<tr><td>2 tablespoons tomato purée</td><td>2 tablespoons tomato paste</td></tr>
<tr><td>½ teaspoon ground coriander</td><td>½ teaspoon ground coriander</td></tr>
<tr><td>salt</td><td>salt</td></tr>
<tr><td>freshly ground black pepper</td><td>freshly ground black pepper</td></tr>
<tr><td>chopped fresh parsley to garnish</td><td>chopped fresh parsley to garnish</td></tr>
</table>

Wipe the mushrooms and leave whole. Thickly slice the aubergine (eggplant), sprinkle with salt and leave for 40 minutes. Rinse under cold running water to remove excess salt, and drain well.

Heat the oil in a large flameproof casserole. Reserving half the mushrooms, add all the other vegetables to the casserole, together with the garlic, tomato purée (paste), coriander, salt and pepper. Stir well to mix thoroughly. Cover and bake in a preheated moderate oven (180°C/350°F, Gas Mark 4) for 50 to 60 minutes, stirring once or twice during cooking. Ten minutes before the end of the cooking time, stir in the reserved mushrooms. Adjust the seasoning and serve, hot or cold, garnished with parsley. This makes a delicious first course. It can also be served as a vegetable accompaniment with roast or grilled (broiled) meat.
Serves 8
Total Calories: 450

Florida Cocktail

METRIC/IMPERIAL
2 large grapefruit
4 oranges
sugar or artificial sweetener to taste
Garnish:
granulated sugar
fresh mint sprigs
1 small orange

AMERICAN
2 large grapefruit
4 oranges
sugar or artificial sweetener to taste
Garnish:
sugar
fresh mint sprigs
1 small orange

With a sharp knife, remove all the skin and pith from the grapefruit and 4 oranges. Cut into the sections down towards the centre of the fruit, discarding all membrane and seeds. Add sugar or artificial sweetener to taste, and chill in the refrigerator.

Frost 4 wine glasses by dipping their rims first in fruit juice and then in sugar. Divide the mixed orange and grapefruit between the 4 glasses. Serve garnished with mint sprigs and a thin slice from the remaining orange, cut without removing the rind.
Serves 4
Total Calories: 110 (without sugar)

Slimmer's Delight

METRIC/IMPERIAL
150 ml/¼ pint low fat natural
  yogurt
1 tablespoon tomato purée
1 tablespoon chopped fresh chives or
  spring onions
salt
freshly ground black pepper
225 g/8 oz button mushrooms
chicory leaves to garnish

AMERICAN
⅔ cup low fat unflavored yogurt
1 tablespoon tomato paste
1 tablespoon chopped fresh chives or
  scallions
salt
freshly ground black pepper
2 cups button mushrooms
Belgian endive leaves to garnish

Place the yogurt, tomato purée (paste), chives and salt and pepper in a bowl and mix thoroughly. Stir in the mushrooms. Spoon on to a bed of chicory (Belgian endive) leaves. Serve with crispbread slices.
Serves 4
Total Calories: 130

Stuffed Vine Leaves

METRIC/IMPERIAL	AMERICAN
1 tablespoon vegetable oil	1 tablespoon vegetable oil
1 medium onion, peeled and chopped	1 medium onion, peeled and chopped
1 clove garlic, crushed	1 clove garlic, crushed
75 g/3 oz chicken livers	½ cup chicken livers
100 g/4 oz cooked rice	⅔ cup cooked rice
25 g/1 oz pine kernels	¼ cup pine nuts
salt	salt
freshly ground black pepper	freshly ground black pepper
36 canned vine leaves	36 canned vine leaves
approx. 300 ml/½ pint chicken stock	approx. 1¼ cups chicken stock

Heat the oil in a frying pan (skillet) and fry the onion and garlic until soft and transparent. Add the chicken livers and fry for a further 3 minutes, stirring, until lightly browned on all sides. Remove the livers from the pan and chop finely. Place the rice in a bowl and add the livers, onion, garlic and pan juices, the pine kernels and salt and pepper to taste. Mix well.

Lay the vine leaves on a work surface with the underside of the leaves uppermost. Put a teaspoonful of the rice mixture on each leaf and roll up, tucking the sides in, to make a neat parcel. Place the leaves, close together, in a casserole, making two or more layers.

Pour in enough stock to come half-way up the sides of the casserole and just cover the vine leaves. Cover and place in a preheated moderate oven (180°C/350°F, Gas Mark 4) for 30 to 40 minutes until cooked through. Serve at once, or leave until cold.

Serves 6
Total Calories: 550

Mackerel Pâté

METRIC/IMPERIAL	AMERICAN
225 g/8 oz smoked mackerel fillets	½ lb smoked mackerel fillets
1 garlic clove, crushed	1 garlic clove, crushed
freshly ground black pepper	freshly ground black pepper
4 teaspoons lemon juice	4 teaspoons lemon juice
4 tablespoons low fat natural yogurt	¼ cup low fat unflavored yogurt

Skin the mackerel fillets and chop roughly. Add the garlic, freshly ground black pepper to taste, the lemon juice and yogurt. Pound the mixture until soft and thoroughly combined. Chill in the refrigerator until required, Serve with hot crisp toast.

Serves 4
Total Calories: 600

STUFFED VINE LEAVES
(Photograph: Knorr Stock Cubes)

FISH

Plaice (Flounder) and Orange Bake

METRIC/IMPERIAL
4 plaice fillets, skinned
grated rind and juice of 1 orange
parsley sprigs to garnish
Filling:
1 small orange, peeled
1 small green pepper, seeded and
  halved
100 g/4 oz cottage cheese
freshly ground black pepper

AMERICAN
4 flounder fillets, skinned
grated rind and juice of 1 orange
parsley sprigs to garnish
Filling:
1 small orange, peeled
1 small green pepper, seeded and
  halved
½ cup cottage cheese
freshly ground black pepper

For the filling, chop half the orange and half the green pepper. Slice the remainder of each for garnish. Combine the chopped orange and green pepper with the cottage cheese and season with the black pepper.

Divide the filling between the fish fillets and roll them up. Place the stuffed fillets in a casserole and pour over the orange juice and rind. Cover and cook in a preheated moderately hot oven (190°C/375°F, Gas Mark 5) for 40 minutes. Garnish with the remaining orange and pepper slices and parsley.
Serves 2
Total Calories: 450

Seafood Exotica

METRIC/IMPERIAL
1 × 350 g/12 oz can asparagus
  spears
4 plaice fillets, skinned
salt
100 g/4 oz peeled prawns
1 teaspoon lemon juice
150 ml/¼ pint dry white wine and
  water, mixed
4 peppercorns
bouquet garni
1 bay leaf
25 g/1 oz dried skimmed milk
  powder
15 g/½ oz cornflour

AMERICAN
1 × ¾ lb can asparagus spears
4 flounder fillets, skinned
salt
⅔ cup peeled shrimp
1 teaspoon lemon juice
⅔ cup dry white wine and water,
  mixed
4 peppercorns
bouquet garni
1 bay leaf
⅓ cup dried skimmed milk solids
2 tablespoons cornstarch

Drain the asparagus spears and divide into 4. Roll them up inside the fish fillets, securing each roll with a wooden cocktail stick. Season with salt. Arrange the fish in a lightly oiled ovenproof dish and scatter over the prawns (shrimp). Add the lemon juice, wine and water, peppercorns, bouquet garni and bay leaf. Cover and cook in a preheated moderate oven (180°C/350°F, Gas Mark 4) for about 30 minutes.

Lift out the fish and prawns (shrimp) onto a warmed serving dish, and keep warm. Strain the cooking liquid and discard the bouquet garni, peppercorns and bay leaf. Pour the strained liquid into a saucepan; add the milk powder (solids) and stir until dissolved. Blend the cornflour (cornstarch) with a little of the liquid in a cup. Bring the liquid in the saucepan to the boil, then stir in the cornflour (cornstarch) mixture. Simmer for 3 to 4 minutes, stirring constantly. Pour over the fish. Serve with new potatoes or boiled rice.
Serves 4
Total Calories: 720

Sole with Pineapple

METRIC/IMPERIAL
4-8 sole or plaice fillets
lemon juice
a little water
French Dressing:
2 tablespoons wine vinegar or
  lemon juice
3 tablespoons corn oil
½ teaspoon dry mustard
salt
freshly ground black pepper
Garnish:
8 slices pineapple
450 g/1 lb new potatoes, cooked
2 tomatoes, skinned and chopped
chopped fresh parsley

AMERICAN
4-8 sole or small flounder fillets
lemon juice
a little water
French Dressing:
2 tablespoons wine vinegar or
  lemon juice
3 tablespoons corn oil
½ teaspoon dry mustard
salt
freshly ground black pepper
Garnish:
8 slices pineapple
1 lb new potatoes, cooked
2 tomatoes, skinned and chopped
chopped fresh parsley

To prepare the dressing, place the vinegar or lemon juice, corn oil, mustard and salt and pepper to taste in a screw-top jar and shake until well mixed.

Skin the fish, season with lemon juice, salt and pepper and cook in a little water until the flesh flakes. Remove from the water and keep warm. Place the pineapple slices under a hot grill (broiler) for a few minutes. Toss the potatoes and tomatoes in a little of the French dressing.

Arrange the fish on a plate and surround with the potatoes and pineapple. Sprinkle the tomatoes on top of the fish and garnish with the chopped parsley.

Serves 4
Total Calories: 1350

SOLE WITH PINEAPPLE
(Photograph: Mazola Pure Corn Oil)

Summer Fish Dish

METRIC/IMPERIAL
4 cod steaks
grated rind and juice of 1 lemon
Sauce:
175 g/6 oz cucumber, diced
150 ml/¼ pint low fat natural
  yogurt
50 g/2 oz cottage cheese
salt
freshly ground black pepper
Garnish:
cucumber slices
parsley sprigs

AMERICAN
4 cod steaks
grated rind and juice of 1 lemon
Sauce:
1 ½ cups diced cucumber
⅔ cup low fat unflavored yogurt
¼ cup cottage cheese
salt
freshly ground black pepper
Garnish:
cucumber slices
parsley sprigs

Place the cod in an ovenproof dish with the lemon rind and juice. Cover and cook in the centre of a preheated moderate oven (180°C/350°F, Gas Mark 4) for 20 to 25 minutes.

Mix the cucumber, yogurt, cottage cheese, salt and pepper together and serve this sauce on top of the fish. Serve garnished with cucumber slices and parsley.

Serves 4
Total Calories: 700

Kedgeree

METRIC/IMPERIAL
350 g/12 oz smoked haddock
100 g/4 oz long-grain rice
1 × 100 g/4 oz packet frozen peas
25 g/1 oz polyunsaturated
  margarine
2 tablespoons skimmed milk
salt
freshly ground black pepper
2 tablespoons chopped fresh parsley

AMERICAN
¾ lb smoked haddock
½ cup long-grain rice
1 × ¼ lb package frozen peas
2 tablespoons polyunsaturated
  margarine
2 tablespoons skimmed milk
salt
freshly ground black pepper
2 tablespoons chopped fresh parsley

Poach the haddock in boiling water for 15 minutes; drain and flake.

Boil the rice in salted water for 15 to 20 minutes, until just tender, then drain well. Cook the peas for 3 minutes in boiling salted water and drain. Mix together the fish, rice and peas.

Melt the margarine in a pan and add the fish mixture, the skimmed milk, salt and pepper to taste, and the chopped parsley. Stirring continuously, cook over a gentle heat for 2 minutes to heat through.

Serves 4
Total Calories: 810

Curried Fish

METRIC/IMPERIAL
*575 g/1 ¼ lb cod fillet, or other
  white fish*
600 ml/1 pint fish stock or water
salt
freshly ground black pepper
*350 g/12 oz mushrooms, minced or
  finely chopped*
*1 small onion, peeled and minced,
  or finely chopped*
4 teaspoons cornflour
2 teaspoons curry powder
*1 tablespoon mango chutney,
  chopped*
Garnish:
watercress sprigs
lemon slices

AMERICAN
1 ¼ lb cod fillet, or other white fish
2 ½ cups fish stock or water
salt
freshly ground black pepper
*3 cups ground or finely chopped
  mushrooms*
*1 small onion, peeled and ground,
  or finely chopped*
4 teaspoons cornstarch
2 teaspoons curry powder
*1 tablespoon mango chutney,
  chopped*
Garnish:
watercress sprigs
lemon slices

Poach the fish in the stock or water, seasoned with salt and pepper.

Put the mushrooms and onion into a shallow pan, season with salt and pepper and cook gently (without fat or liquid) until the juices begin to run; increase the heat and continue cooking until the mixture is dry. Keep hot.

Drain the fish, reserving the stock, and flake lightly. Blend the cornflour (cornstarch) and curry powder and a little of the fish stock. Mix with the remaining fish stock, made up to 450 ml/¾ pint/2 cups with water, if necessary. Bring to the boil, stir in the chutney and simmer for 3 minutes. Mix the fish and sauce together and leave over a gentle heat for a few moments. Adjust the seasoning to taste.

Make a border of the hot mushroom and onion mixture on a warmed serving dish, turn the curry into the middle and garnish the dish with a few sprigs of watercress and lemon slices.
Serves 4 to 6
Total Calories: 530

Cod Creole and Parsley Rice

METRIC/IMPERIAL	AMERICAN
4 cod steaks or cutlets	4 cod steaks or cutlets
1 × 400 g/14 oz can peeled tomatoes	1 × 14 oz can peeled tomatoes
2 onions, peeled and finely chopped	2 onions, peeled and finely chopped
salt	salt
freshly ground black pepper	freshly ground black pepper
pinch of dried thyme	pinch of dried thyme
225 g/8 oz long-grain rice	1 cup long-grain rice
600 ml/1 pint stock	2½ cups bouillon
2 tablespoons chopped fresh parsley	2 tablespoons chopped fresh parsley

Place the cod steaks or cutlets in a casserole. Drain and chop the tomatoes, reserving the juice, and combine with the onion. Season with salt, pepper and thyme. Place the mixture round the cod steaks and pour over the tomato juice. Cover and cook in a preheated hot oven (220°C/425°F, Gas Mark 7) for 25 minutes.

Put the rice and stock (bouillon) into a saucepan, bring to the boil and stir once. Lower the heat until the rice is simmering, cover and cook for 15 minutes, or until the rice is tender and the liquid absorbed. When cooked, fork in the chopped parsley. Serve the parsley rice with the cod steaks.
Serves 4
Total Calories: 1420

Cod Parcels

METRIC/IMPERIAL	AMERICAN
4 cod steaks, or other white fish	4 cod steaks, or other white fish
grated rind and juice of 1 lemon	grated rind and juice of 1 lemon
50 g/2 oz mushrooms, sliced	½ cup sliced mushrooms
1 tablespoon chopped fresh parsley	1 tablespoon chopped fresh parsley
1 tomato, skinned and sliced	1 tomato, skinned and sliced
1 courgette, sliced	1 zucchini, sliced
salt	salt
freshly ground black pepper	freshly ground black pepper

Put the fish onto a piece of foil large enough to wrap round the fish and vegetables. Add the lemon rind and juice, the mushrooms, parsley, tomato and courgette (zucchini), and season with salt and pepper. Wrap the foil over the fish and fold the edges together to seal tightly. Put onto a baking sheet and bake in a preheated moderately hot oven (190°C/375°F, Gas Mark 5) for 20 minutes.
Serves 4
Total Calories: 640

COD CREOLE AND PARSLEY RICE
(Photograph: American Long-Grain Rice)

Cod Peppers

METRIC/IMPERIAL
4 red or green peppers
225 g/8 oz cod fillet
1 small onion, peeled and chopped
350 g/12 oz mushrooms, chopped
salt
freshly ground black pepper
1 teaspoon Angostura bitters
2 teaspoons anchovy essence

AMERICAN
4 red or green peppers
½ lb cod fillet
1 small onion, peeled and chopped
3 cups chopped mushrooms
salt
freshly ground black pepper
1 teaspoon Angostura bitters
2 teaspoons anchovy extract

Blanch the peppers in boiling salted water for 2 minutes, then cool and pat dry. Cut the peppers in half lengthwise and remove the centre core, seeds and pith, leaving the stalk attached.

Place the fish in a pan with the onion and half the mushrooms, and add enough water to almost cover the fish. Season with salt and pepper. Cover the pan and simmer gently until the fish will flake easily. Drain off the liquid, then flake the fish with a fork, mixing in the onion and mushroom. Stir in the Angostura bitters and anchovy essence (extract).

Fill the peppers with the mixture and place in an ovenproof dish. Cover the dish with a sheet of foil and bake in a preheated moderately hot oven (200°C/400°F, Gas Mark 6) for 20 minutes. Open the foil and add the remaining mushrooms, seasoned with salt and pepper. Replace the foil and cook for a further 15 minutes.
Serves 4
Total Calories: 300

Green Collar Trout

METRIC/IMPERIAL	AMERICAN
4 trout	4 trout
4 open mushrooms	4 open mushrooms
120 ml/4 fl oz white wine	1/2 cup white wine
salt	salt
freshly ground black pepper	freshly ground black pepper
575 g/1 1/4 lb button mushrooms, finely chopped	5 cups finely chopped button mushrooms
2 medium onions, peeled and finely chopped	2 medium onions, peeled and finely chopped
1 small green pepper	1 small green pepper
lemon juice to taste	lemon juice to taste
lemon slices to garnish	lemon slices to garnish

Put the fish and the 4 open mushrooms into a shallow ovenproof dish. Pour over the white wine and season with salt and pepper. Cover and poach in a preheated moderately hot oven (190°C/375°F, Gas Mark 5) for about 25 minutes.

Mix together the chopped mushrooms and onions. Cut 4 rings from the green pepper and reserve; then remove the seeds and pith and finely chop the remainder of the pepper. Strain the liquid from the fish into a shallow pan, reserving the large mushrooms. Add the chopped mushrooms, onions and green pepper to the fish liquor. Season with salt, pepper and lemon juice and cook over a moderate heat until all the liquid has evaporated.

Skin the fish, if preferred. Put the mushroom mixture on to a hot serving dish, arrange the fish on top, and put one of the reserved pepper rings on to each fish, as a collar. Serve garnished with slices of lemon and the whole mushrooms cooked with the fish.

Serves 4
Total Calories: 2840

Baked Apple Mackerel

This recipe is equally good made with fresh herrings or pilchards instead of mackerel. Mackerel, herrings and pilchards are all fatty fish, but their fat content varies according to the time of year, being lowest in the winter months. They could be included in the low fat diet as an occasional treat.

METRIC/IMPERIAL
4 fresh mackerel fillets
2 teaspoons made mustard
salt
freshly ground black pepper
450 g/1 lb potatoes, peeled and sliced
1 medium onion, peeled and thinly sliced
1 teaspoon finely chopped fresh sage, or savory or parsley
1 large cooking apple, peeled and sliced
150 ml/¼ pint cider
boiling water

AMERICAN
4 fresh mackerel fillets
2 teaspoons made mustard
salt
freshly ground black pepper
1 lb potatoes, peeled and sliced
1 medium onion, peeled and thinly sliced
1 teaspoon finely chopped fresh sage, or savory or parsley
1 large baking apple, peeled and sliced
⅔ cup hard cider
boiling water

Trim the fish fillets neatly and spread with the mustard. Season with salt and pepper and roll up. Lightly oil an ovenproof dish and cover the bottom with half the sliced potatoes. Scatter over the onion slices and season with salt, pepper and sage. Cover the potatoes and onions with the apple slices and place the mackerel rolls on top. Arrange the remaining potatoes over the fish and season with more salt and pepper. Add the cider and enough boiling water to half fill the dish.

Cover with foil and bake in a preheated moderate oven (180°C/350°F, Gas Mark 4) for 45 minutes. Remove the foil and continue baking for 30 minutes or until the potatoes are golden brown. Serve very hot.
Serves 4
Total Calories: 3240

BAKED APPLE MACKEREL
(Photograph: Apple and Pear Development Council)

Tuna and Grapefruit Slice

METRIC/IMPERIAL

1 × 200 g/7 oz can tuna fish,
  drained of oil
grated rind and juice of ½
  grapefruit
25 g/1 oz dried skimmed milk
  powder
4 tablespoons cold water
50 g/2 oz fresh white breadcrumbs
1 egg, beaten
1 small onion, peeled and grated
½ teaspoon paprika

Garnish:
lettuce
tomato slices

AMERICAN

1 × 7 oz can tuna fish, drained of
  oil
grated rind and juice of ½
  grapefruit
⅓ cup dried skimmed milk solids
¼ cup cold water
1 cup fresh white breadcrumbs
1 egg, beaten
1 small onion, peeled and grated
½ teaspoon paprika

Garnish:
lettuce
tomato slices

Flake the tuna and mix it with grapefruit rind and juice. Mix the milk powder (solids) with the cold water and add to the tuna, together with the breadcrumbs, egg, onion and paprika. Stir well.

Spoon the mixture into a lightly oiled 450 ml/¾ pint/2 cup ovenproof dish. Smooth the top and bake, on a baking sheet, in the centre of a preheated moderate oven (180°C/350°F, Gas Mark 4) for 40 minutes. Turn out carefully onto a plate and cool. Serve cut in slices and garnished with lettuce and tomato.

Serves 4 to 6
Total Calories: 750

MEAT

Beef Stroganoff

METRIC/IMPERIAL	AMERICAN
450 g/1 lb rump steak	*1 lb rump steak*
2 tablespoons cooking oil	*2 tablespoons cooking oil*
1 onion, peeled and chopped	*1 onion, peeled and chopped*
15 g/½ oz flour	*2 tablespoons flour*
salt	*salt*
freshly ground black pepper	*freshly ground black pepper*
pinch of grated nutmeg	*pinch of grated nutmeg*
100 g/4 oz mushrooms, sliced	*1 cup sliced mushrooms*
300 ml/½ pint stock	*1¼ cups bouillon*
4 tablespoons tomato purée	*¼ cup tomato paste*
5 tablespoons low fat natural yogurt	*⅓ cup low fat unflavored yogurt*

Remove the surplus fat from the meat and cut it into 2.5 cm/1 inch strips. Heat the oil in a heavy non-stick saucepan over a medium heat. Add the strips of steak and toss in the oil until brown on all sides. Stir in the onion and flour and season with salt, pepper and nutmeg. Cook for a few minutes, then add the mushrooms, stock (bouillon) and tomato purée (paste). Bring to the boil, stirring, then place in a casserole and cover. Cook in the centre of a preheated moderate oven (180°C/350°F, Gas Mark 4) for 1 hour. Just before serving adjust the seasoning and stir in the yogurt.
Serves 4
Total Calories: 800

Mid-week Steaks

METRIC/IMPERIAL
*450 g/1 lb blade of beef, cut into
  4-8 thin slices*
225 g/8 oz button mushrooms
Marinade:
1 orange
3 tablespoons lemon juice
2 tablespoons corn oil
300 ml/½ pint dry cider
1 carrot, peeled and sliced
1 small onion, peeled and sliced
1 clove garlic, chopped
1 bay leaf
2 parsley sprigs
¼ teaspoon cayenne pepper
small pinch of grated nutmeg
2 cloves

AMERICAN
*1 lb beef steak, cut into 4-8 thin
  slices*
2 cups button mushrooms
Marinade:
1 orange
3 tablespoons lemon juice
2 tablespoons corn oil
1 ¼ cups hard cider
1 carrot, peeled and sliced
1 small onion, peeled and sliced
1 clove garlic, chopped
1 bay leaf
2 parsley sprigs
¼ teaspoon cayenne pepper
small pinch of grated nutmeg
2 cloves

First prepare the marinade. Halve the orange and reserve one half for garnish. Squeeze the remaining half and put the juice into a large saucepan, together with all the other ingredients for the marinade. Bring to the boil and simmer for 5 minutes, then set aside until cold.

Put the meat into the marinade and leave to stand for 12 to 24 hours. Remove the meat and grill (broil) under a fierce heat, allowing 1 to 2 minutes on each side. Meanwhile, strain the liquid from the marinade into a saucepan and poach the mushrooms in it for about 4 minutes. Arrange the meat and the mushrooms on a serving dish and garnish with slices from the reserved half orange.
Serves 4
Total Calories: 990

Beef Paprika

METRIC/IMPERIAL	AMERICAN
1 kg/2 lb lean braising steak	2 lb lean braising steak
25 g/1 oz flour	¼ cup all-purpose flour
2 tablespoons cooking oil	2 tablespoons cooking oil
2 large onions, peeled and sliced	2 large onions, peeled and sliced
2 tablespoons paprika	2 tablespoons paprika
600 ml/1 pint stock	2½ cups bouillon
1 × 400 g/14 oz can peeled tomatoes	1 × 14 oz can peeled tomatoes
salt	salt
freshly ground black pepper	freshly ground black pepper
1 green pepper, seeded and sliced	1 green pepper, seeded and sliced

Remove all fat from the meat, then cut it into small cubes. Toss the meat in the flour until well coated. Heat the oil in a large heavy saucepan and cook the meat until brown on all sides. Add the onions and paprika and cook for 5 minutes; then add the stock (bouillon), tomatoes, with the juice, and salt and pepper. Bring to the boil, cover and simmer over a low heat for 1 hour. Add the green pepper and cook for a further ½ hour, or until the meat is tender.
Serves 6
Total Calories: 1530

Slimmer's Beef

METRIC/IMPERIAL	AMERICAN
450 g/1 lb lean braising steak	1 lb lean braising steak
salt	salt
freshly ground black pepper	freshly ground black pepper
450 g/1 lb tomatoes, sliced, or 1 × 400 g/14 oz can peeled tomatoes	2 cups sliced tomatoes, or 1 × 14 oz can peeled tomatoes
2 large onions, peeled and sliced	2 large onions, peeled and sliced
450 g/1 lb carrots, peeled and sliced	1 lb carrots, peeled and sliced
100 g/4 oz mushrooms (optional)	1 cup mushrooms (optional)
2 tablespoons chopped fresh parsley	2 tablespoons chopped fresh parsley

Trim any excess fat from the meat. Place a piece of cooking foil, about 60 × 45 cm/24 × 18 inches, on a baking sheet; put the meat in the centre and season with salt and pepper. Place the tomatoes, onions, carrots and mushrooms, if used, on top of the meat and season again with salt and pepper. Sprinkle with the chopped parsley, then fold up the sides of the foil and bring the ends over to form a loose parcel, tucking the edges firmly together to seal. Bake in a preheated moderate oven (180°C/350°F, Gas Mark 4) for 2½ hours.
Serves 4
Total Calories: 820

Spiced Meatballs

METRIC/IMPERIAL

675 g/1½ lb minced lean meat,
  cooked
450 g/1 lb cooked rice
3 tablespoons chopped fresh parsley
1-2 teaspoons salt
1 teaspoon paprika
1 teaspoon freshly ground black
  pepper
2 teaspoons Worcestershire sauce
2 eggs, beaten
toasted breadcrumbs for coating
Sauce:
50 g/2 oz polyunsaturated
  margarine
225 g/8 oz potatoes, peeled and
  diced
450 g/1 lb eating apples, peeled and
  diced
1 large onion, peeled and chopped
2 teaspoons curry powder
600 ml/1 pint skimmed milk and
  stock, mixed
50 g/2 oz sultanas
50 g/2 oz salted peanuts
salt

AMERICAN

3 cups ground lean meat, cooked
3 cups cooked rice
3 tablespoons chopped fresh parsley
1-2 teaspoons salt
1 teaspoon paprika
1 teaspoon freshly ground black
  pepper
2 teaspoons Worcestershire sauce
2 eggs, beaten
toasted breadcrumbs for coating
Sauce:
¼ cup polyunsaturated margarine
1⅓ cups peeled and diced potato
4 cups peeled and diced eating
  apples
1 large onion, peeled and chopped
2 teaspoons curry powder
2½ cups skimmed milk and
  bouillon, mixed
⅓ cup seedless white raisins
⅓ cup shelled salted peanuts
salt

Mix the minced (ground) meat, rice and parsley with the salt, paprika, black pepper and Worcestershire sauce. Bind with the beaten eggs and shape the mixture into 5 cm/2 inch balls. Roll the meatballs in toasted breadcrumbs until thoroughly coated. Place them on a greased baking sheet and bake in a preheated moderate oven (180°C/350°F, Gas Mark 4) for 20 minutes, until nicely browned. Serve with the sauce.

   To make the sauce, heat the margarine in a saucepan and fry the potatoes, apple and onion until the onion begins to colour. Add the curry powder and fry for a further 3 minutes. Stir in the mixed skimmed milk and stock (bouillon), then add the sultanas (raisins), peanuts and salt. Simmer gently until the potato is cooked and the sauce thickened. Serve with fluffy boiled rice.
Serves 6
Total Calories: 1980

Beefburgers with Tomato Sauce

METRIC/IMPERIAL
450 g/1 lb lean minced beef
1 onion, peeled and finely chopped
1 clove garlic, crushed
1 tablespoon Worcestershire sauce
2 teaspoons dry mustard powder
½ teaspoon mixed dried herbs
salt
freshly ground black pepper
1 egg, beaten
Sauce:
2 pickled onions, finely chopped
1 large dill pickled cucumber, finely
  chopped
150 ml/¼ pint tomato ketchup
2 teaspoons Worcestershire sauce

AMERICAN
2 cups lean ground beef
1 onion, peeled and finely chopped
1 clove garlic, crushed
1 tablespoon Worcestershire sauce
2 teaspoons dry mustard powder
½ teaspoon mixed dried herbs
salt
freshly ground black pepper
1 egg, beaten
Sauce:
2 pickled onions, finely chopped
1 large dill pickled cucumber, finely
  chopped
⅔ cup tomato ketchup
2 teaspoons Worcestershire sauce

Put the beef into a bowl and add the onion and garlic. Mix in the Worcestershire sauce, mustard, herbs and salt and pepper and stir all the ingredients thoroughly together. Bind with the beaten egg and form into 8 small patties. Cook for 3 to 5 minutes on each side, either in a hot non-stick frying pan (skillet), without fat, or under a hot grill (broiler). Serve with the tomato sauce.

To make the sauce, add the pickled onions and dill cucumber to the tomato ketchup and Worcestershire sauce. Mix well.
Serves 4 to 6
Total Calories: 1240

BEEFBURGERS WITH TOMATO SAUCE
(Photograph: Pointerware (UK) Ltd)

Goulash

METRIC/IMPERIAL	AMERICAN
450 g/1 lb lean stewing steak	*1 lb lean stewing steak*
2 tablespoons cooking oil	*2 tablespoons cooking oil*
15 g/½ oz flour	*2 tablespoons flour*
salt	*salt*
freshly ground black pepper	*freshly ground black pepper*
1 onion, peeled and chopped	*1 onion, peeled and chopped*
1 teaspoon paprika	*1 teaspoon paprika*
pinch of grated nutmeg	*pinch of grated nutmeg*
pinch of mixed herbs	*pinch of mixed herbs*
1 clove garlic, crushed	*1 clove garlic, crushed*
350 g/12 oz tomatoes, skinned and sliced	*1½ cups skinned and sliced tomatoes*
300 ml/½ pint stock	*1¼ cups bouillon*
5 tablespoons low fat natural yogurt	*⅓ cup low fat unflavored yogurt*
chopped fresh parsley to garnish	*chopped fresh parsley to garnish*

Remove all fat and gristle from the meat and cut it into small cubes. Heat the oil in a frying pan (skillet), add the meat and stir over a moderate heat until lightly browned on all sides. Stir in the flour and salt and pepper; then add the onion, paprika, nutmeg, herbs, garlic and tomatoes. Add the stock (bouillon) and bring to the boil.

Pour the stew into a casserole; cover and place in a preheated moderate oven (160°C/325°F, Gas Mark 3) for 2 hours. Just before serving, stir in the yogurt and sprinkle with parsley.
Serves 4
Total Calories: 770

Bitter-sweet Lamb

METRIC/IMPERIAL
1 kg/2 lb lean stewing lamb,
  chopped
1.2 litres/2 pints water
2 tablespoons malt vinegar
Sauce:
4 tablespoons orange marmalade
2 tablespoons tomato ketchup
2 teaspoons dry mustard
grated rind and juice of 1 orange
150 ml/¼ pint stock
2 teaspoons cornflour
1 orange, cut in wedges, to garnish

AMERICAN
2 lb lean stewing lamb, chopped
5 cups water
2 tablespoons malt vinegar
Sauce:
¼ cup orange marmalade
2 tablespoons tomato ketchup
2 teaspoons dry mustard
grated rind and juice of 1 orange
⅔ cup bouillon
2 teaspoons cornstarch
1 orange, cut in wedges, to garnish

Trim the meat, removing all visible fat, then put the pieces into a pan with the water and vinegar and bring to the boil. Cover the pan, reduce the heat and simmer for 15 minutes. Drain the meat and discard the liquid.

To make the sauce, stir together the marmalade, ketchup, mustard, orange rind and juice and the stock (bouillon) in a saucepan. Bring the mixture to the boil and stir in the meat. When all the meat is coated in the sauce, cover the pan, reduce the heat and simmer for 45 minutes until the lamb is tender. When cooked, lift the pieces of lamb into a warmed serving dish. Keep hot.

Blend the cornflour (cornstarch) with a little water to make a smooth paste, then stir in a little of the hot liquid. When the mixture is smooth, pour it into the sauce. Bring the sauce to the boil, stirring constantly, until thickened and smooth. Pour the sauce over the lamb and serve garnished with orange wedges.

Serves 6
Total Calories: 1960

Lamb Provençale

METRIC/IMPERIAL
1 kg/2 lb lean lamb, thinly sliced
  from the leg
salt
freshly ground black pepper
1 tablespoon flour
1 tablespoon cooking oil
1 onion, peeled and finely chopped
225 g/8 oz tomatoes, skinned,
  seeded and chopped
1 small green pepper, seeded and
  sliced
½ tablespoon tomato purée
150 ml/¼ pint white wine
100 g/4 oz mushrooms, thinly
  sliced

AMERICAN
2 lb lean lamb, thinly sliced from
  the leg
salt
freshly ground black pepper
1 tablespoon flour
1 tablespoon cooking oil
1 onion, peeled and finely chopped
1 cup skinned, seeded and chopped
  tomatoes
1 small green pepper, seeded and
  sliced
½ tablespoon tomato paste
⅔ cup white wine
1 cup thinly sliced mushrooms

Pound the lamb slices well to tenderize. Mix a little salt and pepper with the flour and use it to dust the lamb slices. Heat the oil in a saucepan, add the meat and brown quickly. Add the onion, tomatoes, pepper, tomato purée (paste), white wine and mushrooms and cook for 15 minutes over a gentle heat. Adjust the seasoning, if necessary, and serve with plain boiled rice.

Serves 4
Total Calories: 1880

Saffron Lamb

METRIC/IMPERIAL
4 lean lamb chops
1 teaspoon saffron powder
50 g/2 oz mushrooms, chopped
50 g/2 oz dried skimmed milk
  powder
2 tablespoons water
1 teaspoon lemon juice
4 tomatoes to serve

AMERICAN
4 lean lamb chops
1 teaspoon saffron powder
½ cup chopped mushrooms
⅔ cup dried skimmed milk solids
2 tablespoons water
1 teaspoon lemon juice
4 tomatoes to serve

Trim all fat from the chops and grill (broil) them for about 15 minutes on each side, until cooked through. Transfer to a heatproof dish. Mix together the saffron powder, mushrooms, skimmed milk powder (solids), water and lemon juice. Spread this mixture over the chops and grill (broil) for a few more minutes to heat through. Serve with grilled (broiled) tomatoes.

Serves 4
Total Calories: 800

LAMB PROVENÇALE
(Photograph: New Zealand Lamb Information Bureau)

Spicy Kebabs

METRIC/IMPERIAL
*350 g/12 oz leg of lamb, cut into
4 cm/1½ inch cubes*
4 small tomatoes, halved
100 g/4 oz button mushrooms
*1 green pepper, seeded and cut into
2.5 cm/1 inch squares*
8 bay leaves (optional)
Marinade:
*150 ml/¼ pint low fat natural
yogurt*
juice of 1 lemon
2 teaspoons salt
*1 teaspoon freshly ground black
pepper*
1 small onion, grated

AMERICAN
*¾ lb leg of lamb, cut into 1½ inch
cubes*
4 small tomatoes, halved
1 cup button mushrooms
*1 green pepper, seeded and cut into
1 inch squares*
8 bay leaves (optional)
Marinade:
⅔ cup low fat unflavored yogurt
juice of 1 lemon
2 teaspoons salt
*1 teaspoon freshly ground black
pepper*
1 small onion, grated

Trim all visible fat from the meat. Mix all the marinade ingredients together in a bowl; place the meat in the marinade and leave for approximately 24 hours, turning occasionally. Reserve the marinade and thread the cubes of meat on to 4 long or 8 short skewers, alternating with the tomatoes, mushrooms, pepper, and the bay leaves, if used.

Cook under a hot grill (broiler), turning once, for 10 to 15 minutes. Brush the vegetables with the marinade once or twice during cooking, to prevent them drying out. Serve with boiled rice and salad.

Serves 4
Total Calories: 700

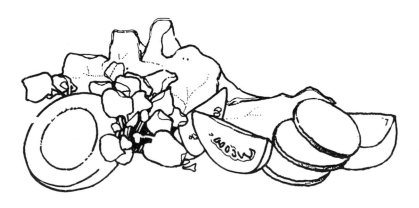

Ham Loaf

METRIC/IMPERIAL	AMERICAN
350 g/12 oz minced lean cooked ham	1½ cups ground lean cooked ham
1 medium onion, peeled and finely chopped	1 medium onion, peeled and finely chopped
40 g/1½ oz fresh white breadcrumbs	¾ cup fresh white breadcrumbs
1 tablespoon chopped fresh parsley	1 tablespoon chopped fresh parsley
2 heaped tablespoons dried skimmed milk powder	2 heaped tablespoons dried skimmed milk solids
½ teaspoon ground mace	½ teaspoon ground mace
salt	salt
freshly ground black pepper	freshly ground black pepper
1 egg, beaten	1 egg, beaten
4 tablespoons water	¼ cup water

Mix together the ham and onion and stir in the breadcrumbs, parsley, skimmed milk powder (solids) and mace. Season with salt and pepper; add the beaten egg and water and mix well.

   Press into a lightly greased 900 ml/1½ pint/3¾ cup casserole. Cover with foil and stand in a roasting pan half-filled with water. Bake in a preheated cool oven (150°C/300°F, Gas Mark 2) for about 45 minutes until cooked. Serve hot or cold, cut into slices.
Serves 4
Total Calories: 760

Sweet and Sour Rabbit

METRIC/IMPERIAL
4 large rabbit joints
1 small carrot, peeled and sliced
1 small onion, peeled and chopped
1 tablespoon cornflour
300 ml/½ pint water
4 teaspoons honey
2 tablespoons soy sauce
2 teaspoons wine vinegar
1 teaspoon ground ginger
salt
freshly ground black pepper
*1 × 225 g/8 oz can pineapple
  chunks, drained*
*1 × 225/8 oz can bean sprouts,
  drained*

AMERICAN
4 large rabbit pieces
1 small carrot, peeled and sliced
1 small onion, peeled and chopped
1 tablespoon cornstarch
1¼ cups water
4 teaspoons honey
2 tablespoons soy sauce
2 teaspoons wine vinegar
1 teaspoon ground ginger
salt
freshly ground black pepper
*1 × ½ lb can pineapple chunks,
  drained*
1 × ½ lb can bean sprouts, drained

Cut the rabbit into small pieces and put them into a large saucepan with the carrot and onion.

Blend the cornflour (cornstarch) with a little of the water to make a smooth paste, then mix with the remaining water in a saucepan. Bring the cornflour (cornstarch) and water to the boil and pour it over the rabbit and vegetables. Add the honey, soy sauce, vinegar and ground ginger and season with salt and pepper. Bring to the boil, cover and simmer for 1½ hours, stirring occasionally, until the rabbit and vegetables are tender.

Add the pineapple chunks and reheat for 5 minutes. Serve immediately with the bean sprouts and boiled rice, if liked.
Serves 4
Total Calories: 890

Tongue Casserole

METRIC/IMPERIAL	AMERICAN
25 g/1 oz polyunsaturated margarine	2 tablespoons polyunsaturated margarine
1 onion, peeled and chopped	1 onion, peeled and chopped
50 g/2 oz bacon, rind and fat removed, and chopped	1/4 cup chopped Canadian bacon slices, fat removed
2 sticks celery, chopped	2 stalks celery, chopped
1 × 225 g/8 oz can peeled tomatoes	1 × 1/2 lb can peeled tomatoes
1 tablespoon Worcestershire sauce	1 tablespoon Worcestershire sauce
150 ml/1/4 pint beef stock	2/3 cup beef bouillon
salt	salt
freshly ground black pepper	freshly ground black pepper
8 lambs' tongues, soaked in cold water	8 lamb tongues, soaked in cold water
2 tablespoons tomato purée	2 tablespoons tomato paste
2 tablespoons cornflour	2 tablespoons cornstarch
3 tablespoons water	3 tablespoons water

Melt the margarine in a pan and fry the onion and bacon gently for 5 minutes. Add the celery and cook for a further 2 minutes. Stir in the tomatoes, Worcestershire sauce and stock (bouillon). Bring to the boil and season with salt and pepper. Pour into a large casserole and arrange the lambs' tongues on top. Cover and cook in a preheated moderate oven (180°C/350°F, Gas Mark 4) for about 2½ hours or until the tongues are tender.

Remove the tongues from the casserole, trim off any bone and remove the skin. Cut each tongue into slices. Skim off any excess fat from the surface of the sauce, then stir in the tomato purée (paste). Blend the cornflour (cornstarch) with the water. Transfer the tomato sauce to a large saucepan; add the cornflour and heat, stirring, until thickened. Cook for 2 minutes, then add the sliced tongues and heat through. Arrange the tongues on a warmed serving dish and coat with the sauce.

Serves 4 to 6
Total Calories: 1200

CHICKEN AND ORANGE CASSEROLE (page 59)
(Photograph: British Poultry Meat Association)

Stuffed Peppers

METRIC/IMPERIAL
4 large green or red peppers
225 g/8 oz onions, peeled and
  chopped
1 clove garlic, crushed
75 g/3 oz long-grain rice
1 litre/1 3/4 pints stock
2 tablespoons tomato purée
1 teaspoon mint sauce
2 teaspoons caster sugar
350 g/12 oz lean cooked lamb,
  diced
salt
freshly ground black pepper

AMERICAN
4 large green or red peppers
2 cups chopped onion
1 clove garlic, crushed
1/2 cup long-grain rice
4 1/4 cups bouillon
2 tablespoons tomato paste
1 teaspoon mint sauce
2 teaspoons sugar
3/4 lb lean cooked lamb, diced
salt
freshly ground black pepper

Cut the tops from the peppers and remove the seeds. Blanch them in boiling water for 3 minutes and drain.

Put the onion, garlic and rice in a saucepan and cover with the stock (bouillon). Add the tomato purée (paste), mint sauce, sugar and lamb and bring to the boil. Cover and simmer for 20 minutes, until the rice is tender and has absorbed all the stock (bouillon). Add salt and pepper to taste.

Stuff the peppers with the rice mixture and place in an ovenproof dish. Cover and bake in a preheated moderate oven (180°C/350°F, Gas Mark 4) for 30 minutes.

Serves 4
Total Calories: 1160

POULTRY

Chicken and turkey are quite low in fat content and are therefore very suitable for the low fat diet. Chicken should be skinned if possible, as the skin is high in cholesterol and fat.

Duck and goose are higher in fat and should be used only very occasionally.

Chicken and Orange Casserole

METRIC/IMPERIAL
2 medium onions, peeled and
  quartered
2 sticks celery, sliced
4 chicken portions, skinned
1 tablespoon chopped fresh herbs
grated rind and juice of 2 oranges
150 ml/¼ pint chicken stock
salt
freshly ground black pepper
Garnish:
1 orange, thinly sliced
watercress

AMERICAN
2 medium onions, peeled and
  quartered
2 stalks celery, sliced
4 chicken portions, skinned
1 tablespoon chopped fresh herbs
grated rind and juice of 2 oranges
⅔ cup chicken bouillon
salt
freshly ground black pepper
Garnish:
1 orange, thinly sliced
watercress

Blanch the onions and celery in boiling salted water for 2 minutes. Put the chicken, celery and onion into a casserole, sprinkle over the herbs, orange rind and juice, and the stock (bouillon). Add salt and pepper to taste. Cover tightly and cook in a preheated moderate oven (180°C/350°F, Gas Mark 4) for about 1 hour, until the chicken is tender. Serve garnished with the orange slices and watercress.
Serves 4
Total Calories: 1000

Gingered Chicken

METRIC/IMPERIAL
2 teaspoons flour
¼ teaspoon powdered ginger
1 × 1 kg/2¼ lb chicken
175 g/6 oz long-grain rice
pinch of saffron
Glaze:
4 tablespoons sliced stem ginger, in
  syrup
1 tablespoon lemon juice
3 tablespoons sherry
15 g/½ oz polyunsaturated
  margarine
Garnish:
almonds
maraschino cherries

AMERICAN
2 teaspoons flour
¼ teaspoon powdered ginger
1 × 2¼ lb chicken
1 cup long-grain rice
pinch of saffron
Glaze:
¼ cup sliced preserved ginger, in
  syrup
1 tablespoon lemon juice
3 tablespoons sherry
1 tablespoon polyunsaturated
  margarine
Garnish:
almonds
maraschino cherries

Mix together the flour and powdered ginger and use to dust the inside of a roasting (browning) bag. Place the chicken in the bag and follow the instructions given with the bag. Cook in a preheated moderately hot oven (200°C/400°F, Gas Mark 6) for 1¼ hours.

Cook the rice in boiling salted water with a little saffron until tender, about 12 minutes.

For the glaze, put the ginger syrup, lemon juice, sherry and margarine into a small saucepan. Bring to the boil and simmer until reduced to a syrup.

When the chicken is cooked, remove from the bag and divide in half lengthways. Arrange the rice on a warmed serving dish and place the chicken on the rice, cooked side uppermost. Pour over the glaze and serve garnished with the sliced ginger, almonds and maraschino cherries.

Serves 4
Total Calories: 1800

GINGERED CHICKEN
(Photograph: Buxted Advisory Service)

Chicken Curry

METRIC/IMPERIAL
1 tablespoon cooking oil
1 medium onion, peeled and finely
  chopped
2 tablespoon curry powder
2 tablespoons flour
450 ml/³/4 pint stock or water
2 teaspoons lemon juice
1 tablespoon mango chutney
150 ml/¹/4 pint low fat natural
  yogurt
1 green eating apple, peeled, cored
  and thinly sliced
50 g/2 oz green seedless grapes
225 g/8 oz cooked chicken, cubed

AMERICAN
1 tablespoon cooking oil
1 medium onion, peeled and finely
  chopped
2 tablespoons curry powder
2 tablespoons flour
2 cups bouillon or water
2 teaspoons lemon juice
1 tablespoon mango chutney
²/3 cup low fat unflavored yogurt
1 green eating apple, peeled, cored
  and thinly sliced
¹/2 cup green seedless grapes
¹/2 lb cooked chicken, cubed

Heat the oil in a frying pan (skillet) and fry the onion until softened. Mix in the curry powder and flour and cook for 1 minute. Gradually blend in the stock (bouillon) or water and cook until thickened, stirring constantly. Add the lemon juice, chutney and yogurt and mix well until creamy. Add the apple and grapes. Finally stir in the chicken, and heat through.
Serves 4
Total Calories: 970

Chicken Dolmades

METRIC/IMPERIAL
8 large green cabbage leaves
100 g/4 oz onion, peeled and finely
  chopped
450 g/1 lb cooked chicken, minced
2 slices white bread, made into
  crumbs
1 teaspoon mixed dried herbs
salt
freshly ground black pepper
pinch of ground ginger
1 × 350 g/12 oz can peeled
  tomatoes
150 ml/¼ pint chicken stock

AMERICAN
8 large green cabbage leaves
1 cup finely chopped onion
2 cups ground cooked chicken
2 slices white bread, made into
  crumbs
1 teaspoon mixed dried herbs
salt
freshly ground black pepper
pinch of ground ginger
1 × 12 oz can peeled tomatoes
⅔ cup chicken bouillon

Remove the coarse centre stem from each cabbage leaf. Plunge the leaves into a pan of boiling salted water and blanch for 2 minutes. Drain thoroughly on absorbent paper.

Mix the onion with the minced (ground) chicken, breadcrumbs, herbs, and salt, pepper and ginger to taste. Form into 8 even-sized balls and wrap each one in a cabbage leaf. Place in a shallow ovenproof dish. Mix the tomatoes with the tomato juice and stock (bouillon) and spoon over them. Cover and cook in a preheated moderate oven (180°C/350°F, Gas Mark 4) for 1 hour.

Serves 4
Total Calories: 900

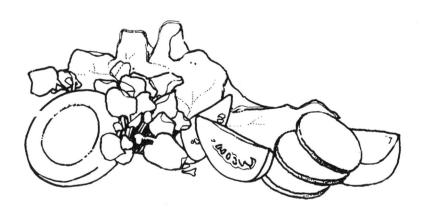

Tandoori Chicken

METRIC/IMPERIAL	AMERICAN
4 chicken portions, skinned	4 chicken portions, skinned
1 teaspoon salt	1 teaspoon salt
2 tablespoons lemon juice	2 tablespoons lemon juice
Marinade:	**Marinade:**
2 tablespoons lemon juice	2 tablespoons lemon juice
2 tablespoons vinegar	2 tablespoons vinegar
2 tablespoons vegetable oil	2 tablespoons vegetable oil
2 tablespoons low fat natural yogurt	2 tablespoons low fat unflavored yogurt
5 teaspoons Tandoori spice mixture	5 teaspoons Tandoori spice mixture
Garnish:	**Garnish:**
lettuce leaves	lettuce leaves
onion rings	onion rings
lemon wedges	lemon wedges

Make several slashes in each chicken portion. Mix together the salt and lemon juice and rub all over the chicken portions. Leave for 30 minutes. Whisk together the marinade ingredients and spoon over the chicken. Cover and leave overnight in a refrigerator.

Drain off the excess marinade and cook the chicken under a hot grill (broiler) for 10 to 15 minutes on each side. Serve with lettuce, onion rings and lemon wedges. Served cold, this makes a good picnic dish.
Serves 4
Total Calories: 760

Chickenburgers

METRIC/IMPERIAL	AMERICAN
225 g/8 oz cooked chicken, minced	1 cup ground, cooked chicken
50 g/2 oz onion, grated	½ cup grated onion
salt	salt
freshly ground black pepper	freshly ground black pepper
1 teaspoon mixed dried herbs	1 teaspoon mixed dried herbs
275 g/10 oz cottage cheese, sieved	1¼ cups cottage cheese, sieved

Mix together the chicken and onion and season with salt and pepper to taste. Add the mixed herbs, then the cottage cheese and mix well. Shape into 4 flat cakes and chill in the refrigerator for 1 hour. Place under a hot grill (broiler) and cook each side for 5 minutes or until golden and heated through. Serve with salad or fresh vegetables.
Serves 4
Total Calories: 690

CHICKEN DOLMADES (page 63)
(Photograph: British Poultry Meat Association)

Chicken with Cider

METRIC/IMPERIAL	AMERICAN
2 tablespoons cooking oil	2 tablespoons cooking oil
4 chicken quarters	4 chicken quarters
225 g/8 oz carrots, peeled and sliced	½ lb carrots, peeled and sliced
2 sticks celery, chopped	2 stalks celery, chopped
450 ml/¾ pint dry cider	2 cups hard cider
2 tablespoons Worcestershire sauce	2 tablespoons Worcestershire sauce
salt	salt
freshly ground black pepper	freshly ground black pepper
2 teaspoons cornflour (optional)	2 teaspoons cornstarch (optional)

Heat the oil in a large frying pan (skillet). Add the chicken quarters and fry quickly until browned, turning once. Remove from the pan, and drain on absorbent paper towels. Place in a large flameproof casserole and add the vegetables, cider, Worcestershire sauce, salt and pepper. Bring to the boil; then cover and cook in a preheated moderate oven (180°C/350°F, Gas Mark 4) for about 1½ hours. Before serving, adjust the seasoning and thicken the sauce with cornflour (cornstarch), if desired.
Serves 4
Total Calories: 880

Chicken Mornay

METRIC/IMPERIAL	AMERICAN
225 g/8 oz cooked chicken meat	½ lb cooked chicken meat
350 g/12 oz cooked spinach	1½ cups cooked spinach
grated rind of ½ lemon	grated rind of ½ lemon
pinch of grated nutmeg	pinch of grated nutmeg
salt	salt
freshly ground black pepper	freshly ground black pepper
300 ml/½ pint low fat natural yogurt	1¼ cups low fat unflavored yogurt
100 g/4 oz Edam cheese, grated	1 cup grated Edam cheese

Brown the chicken lightly on all sides in a non-stick pan. Mix the drained spinach with the lemon rind, nutmeg, salt and pepper, and put into a shallow ovenproof dish. Place the chicken on top. Mix the yogurt with the grated cheese and spoon the mixture over the chicken. Place in a preheated moderately hot oven (190°C/375°F, Gas Mark 5) and bake for 25 to 30 minutes.
Serves 4
Total Calories: 970

VEGETABLES AND SALADS

Vegetable Hot-pot

METRIC/IMPERIAL
25 g/1 oz flour
salt
freshly ground black pepper
2 carrots, peeled and roughly
  chopped
3 onions, peeled and roughly
  chopped
one quarter of a medium swede,
  peeled and roughly chopped
2 sticks celery, diced
4 tomatoes, skinned and chopped
1 × 225 g/8 oz can baked beans
1 teaspoon vegetable extract
600 ml/1 pint stock
3 large potatoes, peeled and sliced
chopped fresh parsley to garnish

AMERICAN
¼ cup flour
salt
freshly ground black pepper
2 carrots, peeled and roughly
  chopped
3 onions, peeled and roughly
  chopped
one quarter of a medium rutabaga,
  peeled and roughly chopped
2 stalks celery, diced
4 tomatoes, skinned and chopped
1 × ½ lb can baked beans
1 teaspoon vegetable extract
2½ cups bouillon
3 large potatoes, peeled and sliced
chopped fresh parsley to garnish

Season the flour with salt and pepper and use to coat the chopped vegetables. Place the vegetables in a large casserole and add the tomatoes and baked beans. Dissolve the vegetable extract in the stock (bouillon) and pour over the vegetables. Cover the top closely with overlapping slices of potato. Bake in a preheated moderate oven (180°C/350°F, Gas Mark 4) for 1 to 1½ hours. Serve sprinkled with chopped parsley.
Serves 5 to 6
Total Calories: 600

Stuffed Tomatoes Italian Style

METRIC/IMPERIAL	AMERICAN
8 large tomatoes	8 large tomatoes
1 tablespoon cooking oil	1 tablespoon cooking oil
1 clove garlic, crushed	1 clove garlic, crushed
1 large onion, peeled and finely chopped	1 large onion, peeled and finely chopped
2 sticks celery, finely chopped	2 stalks celery, finely chopped
100 g/4 oz lean bacon, finely chopped	½ cup finely chopped lean Canadian bacon
50 g/2 oz fresh white breadcrumbs	1 cup fresh white breadcrumbs
1 teaspoon dried oregano or marjoram	1 teaspoon dried oregano or marjoram
4 tablespoons chopped fresh parsley	¼ cup chopped fresh parsley
salt	salt
freshly ground black pepper	freshly ground black pepper
25 g/1 oz grated Parmesan cheese	¼ cup grated Parmesan cheese

Slice the tops off the tomatoes and scoop out, but do not discard, the insides. Heat the oil in a pan, add the garlic, onion, celery, bacon and tomato pulp and cook gently for 5 minutes. Remove from the heat and mix in the breadcrumbs, oregano, parsley, salt and pepper. Fill the tomatoes with this mixture, piling up the stuffing. Sprinkle the tops with cheese; replace the tomato lids and place in a lightly greased ovenproof dish. Cover and bake in a preheated moderate oven (180°C/350°F, Gas Mark 4) for about 20 minutes until tomatoes are cooked. Serve hot or cold.

Serves 4
Total Calories: 600

Cauliflower Cheese

METRIC/IMPERIAL	AMERICAN
1 cauliflower	1 cauliflower
300 ml/½ pint cheese sauce (page 78)	1¼ cups cheese sauce (page 78)
50 g/2 oz Edam cheese, grated	½ cup grated Edam cheese

Cook the cauliflower in boiling water until just tender. Some of the cauliflower water may be used to make up the cheese sauce, but do not add it too hot to the milk powder (solids) or the granules may cook before dissolving.

Put the cauliflower into an ovenproof dish and coat with the sauce. Sprinkle the Edam cheese over the top and brown under a grill (broiler).

Serves 4
Total Calories: 390

CAULIFLOWER CHEESE
(Photograph: Colman's Mustard)

Sweet-sour Red Cabbage

METRIC/IMPERIAL
1 small red cabbage, washed,
  trimmed and thinly sliced
2 medium onions, peeled and thinly
  sliced
2 cooking apples, peeled, cored and
  sliced
2 tablespoons sugar
salt
freshly ground black pepper
bouquet garni of parsley, thyme and
  bay leaf
2 tablespoons red wine or chicken
  stock
2 tablespoons wine vinegar

AMERICAN
1 small red cabbage, washed,
  trimmed and thinly sliced
2 medium onions, peeled and thinly
  sliced
2 baking apples, peeled, cored and
  sliced
2 tablespoons sugar
salt
freshly ground black pepper
bouquet garni of parsley, thyme and
  bay leaf
2 tablespoons red wine or chicken
  bouillon
2 tablespoons wine vinegar

Put the sliced cabbage, onions and apples in alternate layers in a deep earthenware pot, seasoning each layer with a little sugar and salt and pepper. When the pot is full, make a bouquet garni of the parsley, thyme and a bay leaf, tied together with thread, and push this down into the middle of the pot. Pour over the wine or stock (bouillon) and wine vinegar.

Cover the pot with a tight-fitting lid or foil and bake in a preheated cool oven (150°C/300°F, Gas Mark 2) for about 3 hours. This dish reheats very well, and can be stored in the freezer.
Serves 4
Total Calories: 350

Mushroom and Bean Salad

METRIC/IMPERIAL
175 g/6 oz broad beans
225 g/8 oz button mushroooms
4 spring onions, chopped
150 ml/¼ pint low fat natural
  yogurt
salt
freshly ground black pepper

AMERICAN
1 cup lima beans
2 cups button mushrooms
4 scallions, chopped
⅔ cup low fat unflavored yogurt
salt
freshly ground black pepper

Cook the broad (lima) beans in boiling salted water until just tender. Drain and leave to cool. Wipe the mushrooms and slice thinly, leaving the stalks in place. Combine all the ingredients with the yogurt. Season with salt and pepper to taste.
Serves 4
Total Calories: 200

Vegetable Medley

METRIC/IMPERIAL
225 g/8 oz button onions, peeled
225 g/8 oz carrots, peeled and
  halved
225 g/8 oz celery, cut into 10 cm/4
  inch lengths
150 ml/¼ pint water
15 g/½ oz polyunsaturated
  margarine
1 teaspoon salt

AMERICAN
½ lb button onions, peeled
½ lb carrots, peeled and halved
½ lb celery, cut into 4 inch lengths
⅔ cup water
1 tablespoon polyunsaturated
  margarine
1 teaspoon salt

Put a roasting (browning) bag into a large casserole dish. Put the onions, carrots, celery, water and margarine in the bag and season with salt. Close the bag with a twist tie and make six 1 cm/½ inch slits in the top. Cook in a preheated moderate oven (160°C/325°F, Gas Mark 3) for 45 to 60 minutes, or until vegetables are tender.
Serves 5 to 6
Total Calories: 235

Celery with Yogurt Topping

METRIC/IMPERIAL
1 × 400 g/14 oz can celery hearts
4 slices ham, fat removed
Topping:
150 ml/¼ pint low fat natural
  yogurt
50 g/2 oz cucumber, peeled and
  chopped
1 tomato, skinned and chopped
½ teaspoon dried oregano
freshly ground black pepper

AMERICAN
1 × 14 oz can celery hearts
4 slices cooked ham, fat removed
Topping:
⅔ cup low fat unflavored yogurt
½ cup peeled, chopped cucumber
1 tomato, skinned and chopped
½ teaspoon dried oregano
freshly ground black pepper

Put the celery, and liquid, in a saucepan and heat through. Drain well. Wrap a slice of ham around each celery heart and place in an ovenproof dish. Mix together the yogurt, cucumber, tomato, oregano and black pepper, and pour over the celery and ham.

Cover and bake in the middle of a preheated moderate oven (160°C/325°F, Gas Mark 3) for 15 minutes.
Serves 4
Total Calories: 240

Variations:
The celery can be replaced by cooked leeks, chicory or asparagus spears.

Cucumber Rice

METRIC/IMPERIAL
225 g/8 oz long-grain rice
600 ml/1 pint water or chicken
  stock
1 teaspoon salt
1 small cucumber
salt
freshly ground black pepper
chopped fresh dill or parsley

AMERICAN
1 cup long-grain rice
2½ cups water or chicken bouillon
1 teaspoon salt
1 small cucumber
salt
freshly ground black pepper
chopped fresh dill or parsley

Put the rice, water or stock (bouillon) and 1 teaspoon of salt into a saucepan. Bring to the boil and stir once, then lower the heat until simmering. Cover and cook for 15 minutes, or until the rice is tender and the liquid absorbed. Remove from the pan and allow to cool.

Peel the cucumber, halve it lengthways, and scoop out the seeds. Cut it into thick slices and cook, barely covered with water, for 5 minutes. Drain and cool.

Mix together the rice and cucumber, and season to taste with salt, pepper and dill or parsley. Serve with lean cold meat or cold fish.
Serves 4
Total Calories: 830

Peach Salad

METRIC/IMPERIAL
1 × 400 g/14 oz can peach halves
225 g/8 oz cottage cheese
1 tablespoon sultanas
1 tablespoon chopped fresh parsley
  or watercress

AMERICAN
1 × 14 oz can peach halves
1 cup cottage cheese
1 tablespoon seedless white raisins
1 tablespoon chopped fresh parsley
  or watercress

Drain the peaches and rinse in cold water to remove the syrup. Reserve 4 halves. Chop the remaining peach halves and mix with the cottage cheese, sultanas (raisins) and parsley. Pile the cottage cheese mixture into the reserved peach halves and serve with a green salad. Alternatively, divide the mixture between 4 crispbreads and garnish with the sliced peach halves.
Serves 2
Total Calories: 520

Variations:
Other fruits such as fresh apple, orange, grapefruit or pineapple may be used instead of peaches.

CUCUMBER RICE
(Photograph: American Long-Grain Rice)

Curried Mushroom Salad

METRIC/IMPERIAL
225 g/8 oz button mushrooms
100 g/4 oz lean cooked ham,
  chopped
¼ cucumber, diced
150 ml/¼ pint low fat natural
  yogurt
1 teaspoon curry powder
2 teaspoons lemon juice
salt
freshly ground black pepper
2 tablespoons mango chutney

AMERICAN
2 cups button mushrooms
½ cup chopped lean cooked ham
¼ cucumber, diced
⅔ cup low fat unflavored yogurt
1 teaspoon curry powder
2 teaspoons lemon juice
salt
freshly ground black pepper
2 tablespoons mango chutney

Trim the mushrooms and cut any large ones into quarters. Leave small ones whole. Mix together the mushrooms, ham and cucumber in a bowl. Combine the yogurt, curry powder, lemon juice, salt and pepper in a separate bowl. Chop any large pieces of mango in the chutney and add to the yogurt mixture. Add the yogurt mixture to the mushrooms and stir until well coated. Chill in the refrigerator for 1 to 2 hours.
Serves 4
Total Calories: 290

Cheesy Corn on Toast

METRIC/IMPERIAL
1 × 300 g/11 oz can sweetcorn,
  drained
175 g/6 oz cottage cheese
½ teaspoon Worcestershire sauce
salt
freshly ground black pepper
4 large slices wholemeal toast
40 g/1½ oz polyunsaturated
  margarine
4 tomatoes, skinned and sliced

AMERICAN
1 × 11 oz can kernel corn, drained
¾ cup low fat cream cheese
½ teaspoon Worcestershire sauce
salt
freshly ground black pepper
4 large slices wholewheat toast
3 tablespoons polyunsaturated
  margarine
4 tomatoes, skinned and sliced

Place the corn, cottage (low fat cream) cheese, Worcestershire sauce, salt and pepper in a pan and heat gently, stirring occasionally. Spread the toast with a scrape of margarine; lay the tomatoes on top and pile the hot sweetcorn mixture over the tomatoes. Serve immediately.
Serves 4
Total Calories: 920

SWEET AND SAVOURY SAUCES

Creamy Topping

METRIC/IMPERIAL
25 g/1 oz cornflour
300 ml/½ pint skimmed milk
50 g/2 oz polyunsaturated
  margarine
50 g/2 oz sifted icing sugar

AMERICAN
¼ cup cornstarch
1¼ cups skimmed milk
¼ cup polyunsaturated margarine
½ cup sifted confectioners' sugar

Blend the cornflour (cornstarch) with a little of the cold skimmed milk. Heat the remaining milk in a saucepan and pour onto the blended cornflour (cornstarch). Mix well and return to the pan. Bring to the boil and simmer for 1 minute, stirring all the time. Remove from the heat and allow to cool completely, stirring occasionally.

Beat the margarine until soft and gradually work in the icing (confectioners') sugar. Add the cornflour (cornstarch) mixture, a little at a time, beating vigorously to produce a smooth consistency.
Total Calories: 850

Low Calorie Topping

METRIC/IMPERIAL
50 g/2 oz dried skimmed milk
  powder
150 ml/¼ pint ice cold water
2 teaspoons lemon juice
artificial sweetener
vanilla essence

AMERICAN
⅔ cup dried skimmed milk solids
⅔ cup ice cold water
2 teaspoons lemon juice
artificial sweetener
vanilla extract

Mix the milk powder (solids) with the cold water. Add the lemon juice, sweetener and vanilla essence (extract) to taste. Beat hard with a rotary or electric whisk until stiff, then use as required. Serve on fresh fruit salad.

This topping may be made up to ½ hour before it is required.
Total Calories: 190

Tomato Sauce

METRIC/IMPERIAL	AMERICAN
1 tablespoon corn oil	1 tablespoon corn oil
1 onion, peeled and chopped	1 onion, peeled and chopped
2 teaspoons beef stock powder	2 teaspoons beef bouillon powder
1 × 400 g/14 oz can peeled tomatoes	1 × 14 oz can peeled tomatoes
2 teaspoons Worcestershire sauce	2 teaspoons Worcestershire sauce
1 tablespoon cornflour	1 tablespoon cornstarch
150 ml/¼ pint water	⅔ cup water
1 teaspoon salt	1 teaspoon salt

Heat the oil in a frying pan (skillet) and fry the onion until soft and transparent. Add the stock (bouillon) powder, tomatoes and Worcestershire sauce. Blend the cornflour (cornstarch) with a little of the water and add to the pan with the remaining water and the salt. Bring to the boil and simmer for 10 minutes, stirring occasionally.
Total Calories: 280

Salad Dressing

METRIC/IMPERIAL	AMERICAN
pinch of salt	pinch of salt
pinch of sugar	pinch of sugar
pinch of dry mustard	pinch of dry mustard
1 egg white	1 egg white
120 ml/4 fl oz corn oil	½ cup corn oil
2 teaspoons wine vinegar	2 teaspoons wine vinegar
2 teaspoons lemon juice	2 teaspoons lemon juice

Mix together the salt, sugar, mustard and egg white in a bowl. Add half the corn oil, a few drops at a time, whisking throughout. Add the remaining corn oil alternating with the vinegar and lemon juice, to form a creamy consistency.
Total Calories: 950

Tartare Sauce

1 quantity salad dressing (see above)
1 tablespoon chopped gherkins
 (sweet dill pickle)
1 tablespoon capers
1 tablespoon chopped fresh parsley

Mix the salad dressing with the chopped gherkins (dill pickle), capers and parsley and serve with fish. Store in a cool place.
Total Calories: 950

TOMATO SAUCE, TARTARE SAUCE
(Photograph: Mazola Pure Corn Oil)

White Sauce

METRIC/IMPERIAL
50 g/2 oz dried skimmed milk
 powder
600 ml/1 pint water
40 g/1 ½ oz cornflour

AMERICAN
⅔ cup dried skimmed milk solids
2½ cups water
⅓ cup cornstarch

Make up the milk powder (solids) to 600 ml/1 pint/2½ cups with water. Blend a little of the skimmed milk with the cornflour (cornstarch) then add to the rest of the milk and bring to the boil, stirring continuously. Cook briefly.

Add either artificial sweetener and flavouring for a sweet sauce, or salt and pepper for a savoury sauce. This makes a fairly thick coating consistency.
Total Calories: 350

Variations:
For Parsley Sauce: stir 2 tablespoons chopped fresh parsley into savoury white sauce.
For Cheese Sauce: add 50 g/2 oz/½ cup grated Edam cheese and a little mustard to savoury white sauce.

Savoury Sauce

METRIC/IMPERIAL
25 g/1 oz polyunsaturated
 margarine
1 onion, peeled and finely chopped
1 × 400 g/14 oz can peeled
 tomatoes
25 g/1 oz flour
150 ml/¼ pint cider
300 ml/½ pint water
1 beef stock cube
1 tablespoon sugar
2 tablespoons vinegar
1 teaspoon Worcestershire sauce

AMERICAN
2 tablespoons polyunsaturated
 margarine
1 onion, peeled and finely chopped
1 × 14 oz can peeled tomatoes
¼ cup flour
⅔ cup hard cider
1¼ cups water
2 beef bouillon cubes
1 tablespoon sugar
2 tablespoon vinegar
1 teaspoon Worcestershire sauce

Melt the margarine in a frying pan (skillet) and fry the onion gently for 10 minutes. Drain the tomatoes and reserve a little juice to blend with the flour. Chop the tomatoes and add to the onion with the blended flour mixture, cider, water, stock (bouillon) cube(s), sugar, vinegar and Worcestershire sauce. Bring to the boil and simmer for 20 minutes. Serve with grilled (broiled) meat, kebabs or vegetable dishes.
Total Calories: 500

DESSERTS

Although there are many desserts which are not suitable for people on a low fat diet, there are still plenty of sweet dishes which can be enjoyed. This section contains a collection of light desserts which will provide the perfect ending to any meal.

If there is limited time to prepare a dessert, then fresh fruit is the answer, as all fruits, except the avocado pear, are free of fat.

Summer Pudding

METRIC/IMPERIAL	AMERICAN
450 g/1 lb raspberries	3 cups raspberries
450 g/1 lb mixed redcurrants, blackcurrants and strawberries	3 cups mixed redcurrants, blackcurrants and strawberries
75 g/3 oz sugar	6 tablespoons sugar
3 tablespoons water	3 tablespoons water
1 small white sliced loaf, 1 day old	1 small loaf sliced white bread, 1 day old

Prepare and wash the fruit. Place in a pan with the sugar and water, bring to boil and simmer for 1 minute. Leave to cool.

Lightly grease a 1.2 litre/2 pint/5 cup pudding basin (slope-sided mold). Cut the crusts from the bread, reserve 5 slices and cut the remaining slices in half diagonally. Arrange 1 whole bread slice in the bottom of the basin (mold). Closely overlap the bread triangles around the inside of the basin (mold). Fill the centre with fruit, reserving spare juice. Cover the top with the reserved bread slices, cutting the slices if necessary to make them fit. The basin (mold) should be filled to just above the top. Stand on a tray and cover with a plate, slightly larger than the basin (mold). Place a heavy weight on top and leave overnight in the refrigerator or a cold place.

To serve, turn out onto a deep plate and pour over the reserved juice. Serve with low fat natural (unflavored) yogurt.
Serves 6
Total Calories: 1000

Honey Lemon Whip

METRIC/IMPERIAL
150 ml/¼ pint low fat natural
 yogurt
1½ tablespoons clear honey,
 warmed
grated rind and juice of ½ lemon
1 egg white
lemon rind to decorate

AMERICAN
⅔ cup low fat unflavored yogurt
1½ tablespoons clear honey,
 warmed
grated rind and juice of ½ lemon
1 egg white
lemon rind to decorate

Mix together the yogurt, honey, lemon rind and juice. Whisk the egg
white until stiff, then fold into the yogurt mixture. Spoon into 3
individual glasses and decorate with curls of lemon rind. Chill in the
refrigerator and serve soon after making.
Serves 3
Total Calories: 190

Peach Perfection

METRIC/IMPERIAL
1 × 425 g/15 oz can peach slices
2 teaspoons gelatine
2 tablespoons hot water
1 tablespoon lemon juice
1 orange
7 tablespoons instant low fat
 skimmed milk powder
glacé cherries to decorate (optional)

AMERICAN
1 × 15 oz can peach slices
2 teaspoons gelatin
2 tablespoons hot water
1 tablespoon lemon juice
1 orange
7 tablespoons instant low fat
 skimmed milk solids
candied cherries to decorate
 (optional)

Drain the peaches, reserving the juice. Dissolve the gelatine in the
hot water, then make up to 300 ml/½ pint/1¼ cups with peach juice,
lemon juice and water, if necessary. Grate the orange rind into the
liquid, then peel the orange with a sharp knife, and add the chopped
segments to the mixture. Whisk in the skimmed milk powder
(solids) and continue whisking until thick and creamy. Save a few
peach slices for decoration and chop the remainder. Fold the chopped
peaches into the mixture. Pour into a glass serving dish and leave to
set. Decorate with the reserved peach slices and glacé (candied)
cherries, if liked.
Serves 4 to 6
Total Calories: 670

HONEY LEMON WHIP
(Photograph: Gales Honey)

Low Fat Yogurt

It is easy to make low fat yogurt using instant dried skimmed milk powder (solids). If a vacuum flask is used, it is most important to sterilize all equipment, otherwise the yogurt will be very thin. Freezing homemade yogurt is not recommended.

METRIC/IMPERIAL
600 ml/1 pint water
8 heaped tablespoons skimmed milk
  powder
1½ tablespoons commercial low fat
  natural yogurt
large, wide-necked vacuum flask

AMERICAN
2½ cups water
8 heaped tablespoons skimmed milk
  solids
1½ tablespoons commercial low fat
  unflavored yogurt
large, wide-necked vacuum flask

Boil the water, pour into a clean container, cover and leave for 2 hours.

Using boiling water, sterilize a bowl, whisk, tablespoon, the vacuum flask and its cover, and cover until required.

Using the sterilized equipment, measure the skimmed milk powder (solids) into the bowl, whisk in the cooled boiled water and yogurt, pour into the vacuum flask, seal with the stopper and leave undisturbed overnight. 1½ tablespoons of the homemade yogurt can be kept to start another batch, but it is a good idea to revert to commercially produced yogurt occasionally.
Note: Flavours may be added, but will increase the calorie content of the yogurt.
Total Calories: 200

Flavoured Yogurt

To 150 ml/¼ pint/⅔ cup homemade yogurt add any of the following:

15 g/½ oz/1 tablespoon chopped
  hazelnuts
1 tablespoon concentrated orange
  squash
1 teaspoon drinking chocolate,
  dissolved in 1 teaspoon boiling
  water
1 heaped tablespoon canned fruit,
  without juice
any fresh fruit, peeled and chopped
2 teaspoons jam

Plum Snow

METRIC/IMPERIAL
450 g/1 lb plums
3 tablespoons cold water
artificial sweetener to taste
150 ml/¼ pint low fat natural
  yogurt
10 g/¼ oz gelatine
1 tablespoon hot water
1 egg white

AMERICAN
1 lb plums
3 tablespoons cold water
artificial sweetener to taste
⅔ cup low fat unflavored yogurt
½ envelope gelatin
1 tablespoon hot water
1 egg white

Cook the plums with the cold water until soft. Drain off the water, remove the stones (pits) and push the fruit through a coarse sieve. Sweeten the fruit to taste with artificial sweetener, and allow to cool slightly. Beat in the yogurt.

Dissolve the gelatine in the hot water and gradually stir it into the mixture. Beat the egg white until stiff and fold it in. Pile into 4 individual glasses and leave to cool and set.

Serves 4
Total Calories: 200

Malvern Puddings

METRIC/IMPERIAL
450 g/1 lb cooking apples, peeled,
  cored and sliced
4 tablespoons water
1 teaspoon ground cinnamon
1 teaspoon ground mixed spice
artificial sweetener
1½ tablespoons custard powder
300 ml/½ pint skimmed milk
25 g/1 oz cornflakes
15 g/½ oz chopped nuts

AMERICAN
1 lb baking apples, peeled, cored
  and sliced
¼ cup water
1 teaspoon ground cinnamon
1 teaspoon ground mixed spice
artificial sweetener
1½ tablespoons custard powder
1¼ cups skimmed milk
¼ cup cornflakes
1 tablespoon chopped nuts

Stew the apples gently in the water, with half the cinnamon and mixed spice. When cooked, sweeten to taste with artificial sweetener. Divide the apple between 6 individual heatproof dishes. Make up the custard with the skimmed milk, sweetening with artificial sweetener as necessary; pour over the apple. Lightly crush the cornflakes, mix with the nuts and remaining spice, then divide between the dishes. Grill (broil) quickly until golden brown, then serve immediately.

Serves 6
Total Calories: 550

Meringue Cake

METRIC/IMPERIAL
2 teaspoons oil
4 egg whites
225 g/8 oz caster sugar
450 g/1 lb fresh fruit in season
  (strawberries, raspberries,
  peaches, apricots), or 1 × 400 g/
  14 oz can of fruit, drained of juice

AMERICAN
2 teaspoons oil
4 egg whites
1 cup sugar
1 lb fresh fruit in season
  (strawberries, raspberries,
  peaches, apricots), or 1 × 14 oz
  can of fruit, drained of juice

Lay a piece of cooking foil, 30 cm/12 inches square, on a baking sheet and make out a 20 cm/8 inch circle. Brush the foil with oil.

Beat the egg whites until they are very stiff and stand in peaks. Gradually beat in half the sugar, a teaspoon at a time, then fold in the remainder. Spread half the meringue over the circle, taking it right to the edges. Using a dessertspoon, pile spoonfuls of meringue all round the edge to make a case. Bake in a very cool oven (110°C/225°F, Gas Mark ¼) for about 6 hours, or until the meringue has completely dried out. Allow to cool, then peel off the foil.

Fill the centre of the mergingue cake with fruit and serve alone or with Low Calorie or Creamy Topping.
Serves 6
Total Calories: 1040

Orange and Banana Compote

METRIC/IMPERIAL
2 oranges
4 bananas
2 tablespoons lemon juice
1 egg white
150 ml/¼ pint mandarin-flavoured
  yogurt

AMERICAN
2 oranges
4 bananas
2 tablespoons lemon juice
1 egg white
⅔ cup orange-flavored yogurt

Remove the peel and pith from the oranges, using a sharp knife. Slice the oranges and place in a small bowl. Peel and slice the bananas and toss in the lemon juice. Cover and leave to stand for 30 minutes.

Reserve 4 slices of orange for decoration and layer the remaining orange slices and banana in 4 sundae dishes. Beat the egg white until stiff and fold gently through the yogurt. Pour the mixture into the sundae dishes and decorate with a twist of orange.
Serves 4
Total Calories: 480

MERINGUE CAKE
(Photograph: Bacofoil Information Service)

Blackberry Mousse

METRIC/IMPERIAL
450 g/1 lb cooking apples, peeled,
  cored and sliced
100 g/4 oz blackberries
100 g/4 oz sugar
150 ml/¼ pint water
juice of 1 lemon
15 g/½ oz gelatine
2 egg whites

AMERICAN
1 lb baking apples, peeled, cored
  and sliced
1 cup blackberries
½ cup sugar
⅔ cup water
juice of 1 lemon
1 envelope gelatin
2 egg whites

Put the apples in a saucepan with the blackberries, half the sugar and the water. Cover and simmer for 10 to 15 minutes, until tender. Strain the lemon juice into a small bowl and sprinkle the gelatine onto it. Leave to soak.

Rub the fruit and its juice through a coarse sieve into a bowl, discarding the seeds. Dissolve the gelatine in the hot fruit purée and mix well. Leave until the purée is cold and beginning to thicken, then quickly beat the egg white with the remaining sugar and fold into the purée. Turn into individual dishes and chill until set.
Serves 4
Total Calories: 640

Orange Rice Pudding

METRIC/IMPERIAL
50 g/2 oz pudding rice
600 ml/1 pint skimmed milk
grated rind of 1 orange
pinch of grated nutmeg
2 egg whites
50 g/2 oz caster sugar

AMERICAN
4 tablespoons dessert rice
2½ cups skimmed milk
grated rind of 1 orange
pinch of grated nutmeg
2 egg whites
¼ cup sugar

Place the rice, skimmed milk, grated orange rind and nutmeg in a saucepan and cook over a very low heat for 1½ to 2 hours, stirring occasionally. When the rice is tender, pour into a serving dish. Whisk the egg whites to a soft peak, fold in the sugar and spread or pipe over the rice. Place under a hot grill (broiler) until lightly browned. Serve immediately.
Serves 4
Total Calories: 600

Raspberry Sorbet

METRIC/IMPERIAL
600 ml/1 pint water
artificial sweetener
grated rind and juice of 1 lemon
350 g/12 oz raspberries
2 egg whites

AMERICAN
2½ cups water
artificial sweetener
grated rind and juice of 1 lemon
2½ cups raspberries
2 egg whites

Simmer the water, artificial sweetener to the equivalent of 225 g/8 oz/ 1 cup sugar, the lemon rind and raspberries for 10 minutes. Leave to cool. Add the lemon juice and pour into an empty ice cube tray. Leave to half-freeze in the ice compartment of the refrigerator or in the freezer. When the sorbet is in a grainy, half-frozen state, empty it into a bowl. Beat the egg whites until stiff and add to the sorbet, mixing thoroughly. Freeze until firm.
Serves 5 to 6
Total Calories: 100

Baked Pears

METRIC/IMPERIAL
4 ripe pears
150 g/5 oz cranberry sauce
4 tablespoons red wine or water
¼ teaspoon ground cinnamon

AMERICAN
4 ripe pears
⅔ cup cranberry sauce
¼ cup red wine or water
¼ teaspoon ground cinnamon

Cut the pears in half lengthways, peel and remove the core. Blend the cranberry sauce, red wine or water and cinnamon together in a saucepan. Add the pears, cover the pan and cook gently until the pears are tender. Lift out the pears onto a serving plate. Allow the sauce to cool until it becomes syrupy, then spoon over the pears to coat. Serve chilled.
Serves 4
Total Calories: 530

CAKES

Most cake and biscuit (cookie) recipes contain quite a lot of fat and are therefore not suitable on a low fat diet. It is possible to bake with oil or polyunsaturated margarine instead of saturated fat, but if you are trying to limit your total fat intake it is sensible not to have even these cakes and biscuits (cookies) too often. In this section are just 3 cake recipes, which contain no fat at all. The Angle Cake recipe could be served with fruit and jelly (jello), and the Fig Loaf and Bran Fruit Loaf could be an occasional teatime treat.

Fig Loaf

METRIC/IMPERIAL
100 g/4 oz All-Bran
100 g/4 oz dark soft brown sugar
100 g/4 oz dried figs, chopped
2 teaspoons black treacle
300 ml/½ pint skimmed milk
100 g/4 oz self-raising flour

AMERICAN
1½ cups All-Bran
⅔ cup dark soft brown sugar
¾ cup chopped dried figs
2 teaspoons molasses
1¼ cups skimmed milk
1 cup self-rising flour

Put the All-Bran, sugar, figs, black treacle (molasses) and skimmed milk into a bowl. Mix well together and leave to stand for half an hour. Sift in the flour, mixing well. Put the mixture into a greased 450 g/1 lb loaf tin and bake in a preheated moderate oven, (180°C/350°F, Gas Mark 4) for 45 to 60 minutes. Turn out of the tin and allow to cool. If you like, serve sliced, and spread with polyunsaturated margarine.
Total Calories: 1350

FIG LOAF
(Photograph: The Kellogg Company of Great Britain Ltd)

Bran Fruit Loaf

METRIC/IMPERIAL
100 g/4 oz All-Bran, or Bran Buds
150 g/5 oz caster sugar
275 g/10 oz mixed dried fruit
300 ml/½ pint skimmed milk
100 g/4 oz self-raising flour

AMERICAN
1½ cups All-Bran, or Bran Buds
⅔ cup sugar
2 cups mixed dried fruit
1¼ cups skimmed milk
1 cup self-rising flour

Put the All-Bran, sugar and dried fruit into a bowl, mix them well together and stir in the skimmed milk. Leave to stand for half an hour. Sift in the flour, mixing well and pour the mixture into a greased 900 g/2 lb loaf tin. Bake in a preheated moderate oven (180°C/350°F, Gas Mark 4) for about 1 hour. Turn out of the tin and allow to cool. If you like, serve sliced, and spread with a little polyunsaturated margarine.
Total Calories: 2000

Angel Cake

METRIC/IMPERIAL
50 g/2 oz plain flour
125 g/4½ oz caster sugar
150 ml/¼ pint egg whites
pinch of salt
½ teaspoon cream of tartar
½ teaspoon vanilla essence

AMERICAN
½ cup all-purpose flour
½ cup sugar
⅔ cup egg whites
pinch of salt
½ teaspoon cream of tartar
½ teaspoon vanilla extract

Use an ungreased 15 cm/6 inch sandwich tin (layer cake pan) or a tube pan. Sift the flour and sugar separately 3 times; then sift the flour with a quarter of the sugar. Put the egg whites and salt in a large, clean, dry bowl and whisk until frothy. Sprinkle on the cream of tartar and continue whisking until the white stands up in peaks. Avoid overwhisking to a point when the white loses its glossiness.

Lightly beat in the rest of the sugar and the vanilla essence (extract). Using a tablespoon, carefully and gradually fold in the sifted flour and sugar. Pour into the ungreased cake tin and gently cut through the mixture with a knife to release the air bubbles. Bake for 40 to 45 minutes in a preheated cool oven (140°C/275°F, Gas Mark 1) increasing the heat to 160°C/325°F, Gas Mark 3 for the last 10 to 15 minutes. Allow the cake to stand for 30 minutes in the inverted tin, then turn out on to a cooling tray. (When the top springs back on finger pressure the cake is cooked.)
Total Calories: 690

INDEX

INDEX

PDO 81-755

Painted Furniture

RICHARD WILES

BROCKHAMPTON PRESS
LONDON

For Jemima and Orlando

A WARD LOCK BOOK

First published in the UK 1995
by Ward Lock
Wellington House
125 Strand
London
WC2R 0BB

A Cassell Imprint

Text © Richard Wiles 1995
Photographs © Houses & Interiors 1995
Illustrations © Ward Lock 1995

This edition published 1998 by Brockhampton Press.
a member of Hodder Headline PLC Group

ISBN 1 86019 883X

A British Library Cataloguing in Publication Data block for this book may be obtained from the British Library

Typeset by Litho Link Ltd, Welshpool, Powys, Wales

Printed at Oriental Press, Dubai, U.A.E.

contents

Painting your own items of furniture is one of the best ways to add individuality to your home. It allows you to revive flagging, shabby chairs, tables, chests, dressers and other pieces, perhaps bought for a song in junk shops, or cheap modern items purchased with economy in mind, and invest them with a bright new finish that is also unique.

Special paint effects can be subtle and sophisticated, flamboyantly quirky, graphically neat, or cutely pretty, and the furniture used for the projects in this book was chosen especially to demonstrate the versatility of paint treatments. You can begin by following the step-by-step instructions for one or more of the smaller, simpler projects, moving on to the more advanced techniques as you gain in experience and confidence. Then use the wealth of ideas and inspirational photographs as a springboard for developing your own projects and decorative schemes – the choice is yours and the possibilities almost endless, although guidance is given on selecting the colours, themes and techniques which will best suit both you and your home and help you to create your own unique style.

None of the projects used here will take more than a few hours to complete, including the time spent on preparation – a must for best results – while all the methods described make use of paints, varnishes and other materials which are readily available from decorating shops and do-it-yourself stores. You certainly do not have to search out ingredients and blend them carefully in the manner of the true craftsman, and the range of specialist tools and other equipment you will need is decidedly minimal and often disposable.

With all the paint effects included in this book the emphasis is on economy, speed and ease of application, but the results are stunningly effective – with a professional finish that will enhance any decorative scheme and every room in the home.

The simple shapes and muted colours of the patterns on crockery and ethnic rug are picked up in the painted decoration of a floor-standing plate rack, unifying the disparate elements in this dining-room corner.

C R E A T I N G   A   S T Y L E

The mood or atmosphere in particular rooms in your home is largely determined by the overall decorative treatment you choose to apply, in conjunction with your selection of furniture, soft furnishings and accessories. Depending upon the style and age of the furniture, the materials from which it is made and, of course, the way in which it has been finished and decorated, you can evoke a host of diverse moods and themes – whether it be a rustic country air, sleek modern styling, a sumptuous, sophisticated feel, or an atmosphere rich in quirky and flamboyant humour.

The paint techniques and complete projects included in this book make use of a wide range of themes and styles which are easy to achieve, yet excitingly original. This chapter will guide you through the basic principles of creating a style for your own home, into which a project or technique that appeals to you can be incorporated. It also discusses examples of different styles and schemes to act as starting points for your own thoughts and ideas, while the pieces depicted in the colour photographs provide a further source of design inspiration and demonstrate how painted furniture can act as a focal point, highlight or unifying element in an existing scheme or a scheme in preparation.

A SUITABLE BACKDROP

It is important to remember that not all special paint effects will be successful on all types of furniture, nor will they necessarily enhance every decorative scheme. Bear in mind that furniture – apart from being practical, and essential to your comfort and convenience – is an accessory to the basic shell of the room, and it is the shape, size and style of the room which is largely responsible for the success of the decorative treatment. Nevertheless, careful selection of these accessories, and the way in which they complement the room, is essential: a look through the photographs in this chapter and in the project section will demonstrate how a successful choice of design and finish for a piece or pieces of furniture can make all the difference to the overall effect of a scheme.

When you are deciding on how to decorate your home, it is best if you can start with a blank canvas. If it is practicable, you should try to live with an undecorated shell until you get the feel for what you would like to achieve. It is a good idea to strip off all traces of previous paint finishes, wall- and floor-coverings in order to create this blank canvas. Paper the walls with plain lining paper, which will give a smooth, flat surface on which to decorate. Obviously, this is easier if you have just moved into a new house, or have already decided on a complete redecoration programme.

SOURCES FOR STYLE

There are almost unlimited sources of inspiration and information for styling your home: study glossy interiors and style magazines, holiday brochures, beautiful coffee-table books, newspapers, even product packaging, to help you create decorative schemes that reflect your personality and taste.

At the same time, think about how your furniture can be arranged within the room to best effect. Be theatrical in the way you display furniture and ornaments; be bold – but be sensitive. Consider the scale of furniture in relation to the size and shape of the room and choose styles that will not be at odds with other possessions. Your source materials will be invaluable in helping you to arrive at a scheme which works.

Be practical, too, because you have to live with the end result of your efforts. If you embark on too minimalist a treatment, you might find the overall effect austere and unwelcoming; if your treatment is too cluttered, you may well find the result claustrophobic – and a nightmare to keep clean and dust free.

There are innumerable different atmospheres you can create with your decorative schemes and the following is a brief selection of the definitive ideas to whet your appetite and to act as a springboard for evolving your own particular environment for living.

Ethnic quality

To infuse your rooms with an ethnic quality, decorate items of furniture with naïve or primitive symbols based on designs commonly found on artefacts from exotic lands and ancient cultures, such as Africa, Mexico, Greece and China. Study and duplicate the colours, textures and motifs used to adorn simple artisan furniture, which you can often pick up cheaply in junk shops, antique and bric-à-brac stores, and accessorize accordingly.

Freehand-painted motifs and designs, impressed using a variety of different objects – including fruit, vegetables and other everyday household items, in addition to paint rollers, pads or brushes – will suit the almost childlike innocence of this treatment, as will combed and dragged effects. The hall stand on page 72, for example, demonstrates how a simple treatment of alternating series of wavy and angular lines combed in thick, orangy glaze over a dark terracotta basecoat can look distinctly African in influence.

When accessorizing an ethnic-style treatment, terracotta

plantholders holding spiky cacti, succulents or exotic-looking blooms look particularly authentic, especially when placed next to a Mexican-style item of furniture, such as the corner cupboard shown on page 58. Leave the pots in their original terracotta finish, or paint them in brilliant white emulsion and decorate with symbols in brick red, sun yellow, rusty orange or deep blue.

Seek out articles that will adorn your furniture and enhance its ethnic quality, such as the bowl containing acorns and exotic seedpods in the corner cupboard on page 57.

Mediterranean feel

Used in your home, the bright colours of the Mediterranean will bring to mind memories of the hot climates of countries such as Spain, Italy and Greece. For example, the vivid blues, greens and reds of little Greek fishing boats offset against the brilliance of whitewashed, stuccoed houses and the deep blue of the sea can be used to decorate your home and furniture with great success. Alternatively, the faded browns and mellow yellows of noble but crumbling Italian buildings give the appearance of a patina that only time can bring about, and sponged, stencilled, dragged or freehand-painted techniques complement this setting most successfully.

Accessorize with beachcombed relics, such as driftwood, rounded stones from the sea, starfish and shells, or mementoes of holidays, such as model fishing boats, painted ceramics, ecclesiastical icons or local handicrafts that suggest a particular region. Lush plants such as pelargoniums can live happily indoors in large, rounded terracotta pots. Again, cacti and succulents complement this theme, as does the beautiful purple- or red-flowered bougainvillaea, which thrives as an outdoor climber in warmer countries and can be grown indoors in more temperate climates.

Cottagey air

The greens and browns of the countryside, the primary brilliance of fresh blooms and the papery delicacy of dried flowers and foliage each suggest a quaint, cottagey feeling which can soften the hard lines of many items of furniture and some decorative schemes. Floral and foliage motifs, twisting stems and items gleaned from nature – nuts, berries and seedpods – can lend a distinctly rural atmosphere to a scheme, particularly when stencilled on to furniture, walls and floors.

The muted tones and textures of sponged colouring and designs also complement this theme perfectly, as demonstrated on the petite plant stand shown on page 48, featuring finely painted fronds of ivy curling around the legs, with sponge-stencilled leaves in tones of green. In a similar way, the innocently rendered freehand designs of artisan furniture help to create a rural feeling. The country-style plate

Opposite:

The rustic charm of this green chest of drawers, with contrasting trim, adds to the cool, serene effect of this simple bedroom. Note how the colours of the chest are echoed in the treatment of the mirror and the lamp.

rack featured on page 56, for instance, is adorned with stems and berries hanging in garlands, while a streaky red line picks out the moulded, curved front of the piece.

Accessories for a country setting are quite easy to obtain from junk and antique shops or car-boot sales. Collections of butter and cheese dishes, jugs and sugar bowls, and salt-and-pepper sets resembling little cottages, are wonderfully rustic in appearance, while embroidered pictures, samplers and baskets full of dried flowers are the perfect complement to the country style.

City scape

Glitzy colours, smooth, shiny textures, metal and glass are evocative of the lively city landscape, and can be applied to furniture and furnishings to infuse a vibrancy into your decor. Coloured lacquers sprayed on to smooth surfaces, light-reflecting metallic paints and sparkling, glittery motifs will enhance an otherwise plain, minimalist backdrop of walls and floors.

Spattered paint effects in particular look good when applied to plain, uncompromisingly modern furniture and allow you to experiment with bold, brash, often complementary colours. The effect shown on page 32, for example, demonstrates the use of flicked-on paint and a daring choice of colours: a moderate spattering of mauve, blue and green on a pale blue tabletop contrasts starkly with the bold use of richer tones for wall, dado and floor, transforming a cheap round chipboard table into a stunningly modern focal point.

Less brash treatments can still be used to give a modern appearance: false graining on a plain, self-assembly, flat-packed melamine cabinet, as shown on page 53, will look particularly fresh if the choice of colour is not naturalistic. Again, using a combed paint effect, such as that on the kitchen unit shown on page 73, is undeniably modern, but with a hint of the traditional.

Accessories for a modern setting can be minimal in the extreme: a vase of astonishingly false-looking gazanias in gaudy colours, for instance, is virtually all that is needed to complete – and somewhat soften – the picture of the round table mentioned above. Choice of glassware, as with the drinks cabinet, should be influenced by simplicity of shape, with little or no other colour involved. The plainer the item is, the more modern the overall appearance of the furniture will be. Other accessories for a modern touch can be blatantly primary-coloured plastic, shiny, reflective chrome or matt black or primary colours for ornaments and items of furniture.

Jazzy and jaunty

Adopting a sense of humour is important if you intend to create enjoyable settings for living in – and you can also have immense fun while creating them. Harking back to past eras is an ideal starting point: the graphic quality of 1950s and 1960s styling, for example, can be ideally rendered with impressed patterns or rollered designs, and the motifs which proliferated reflect the liveliness of the period. Regularity and economy of pattern is important, as is the careful and modest selection of colours. The jazzy trolley shown on page 37, for instance, uses only black and yellow to create a lively checkerboard effect, transforming what was a fairly boring, outdated piece into a quirky and useful item of furniture.

Another example of humour is the lined hall table shown on page 77, which was rollered in tones of grey to resemble a checked cotton cloth thrown over the top; likewise, a more bizarre lined effect is applied to a playroom bookshelf with daubs of multi-coloured lines creating a riot of jolly colour (see page 76).

More subtle, yet just as effective, is the shoal of little fishes swimming across the blue-sprayed Lloyd-loom chair in a bathroom with a nautical theme, which is shown on page 41. Accessories for such a scheme suggest themselves, with items gleaned from, or evocative of, the seaside.

If you are using a particular era as a starting point for your scheme, then accessorize in the style of the period: black-and-white pictures on the walls and items such as old-style radios, record albums from the era and Bakelite desk fans.

THE KEY TO SUCCESS

The above are just a few examples of ways in which themes and styles can be built up to create an overall decorative scheme. It is easy, however, to get carried away. Decorating absolutely every piece of furniture in your room with a special paint effect could be disastrous; an overkill of one specific technique used on chairs, tables, cabinets and other items would probably result in the originality of the effect being lost – you simply wouldn't appreciate it.

Be selective in your use of paint effects, decorating, say, just a single distinctive chair with an impressed pattern or dragged finish. In that way, the piece will have great originality and interest and form a focal point for the room.

In the same way, it would be unwise to employ too many different paint effects on a range of items in the same room: the luxurious appearance of marbling may not blend especially well with the simplicity of a naïve freehand paint effect, while jazzy impressed patterns would not necessarily sit happily next to a rustic wood-grain simulation. By the same token, don't mix wholly diverse styles of furniture in one scheme – a 1950s tea trolley with blotchy random patterning would not enhance the rural charm of a plate rack adorned with scrolling ivy stems and leaves.

PRACTICALITIES

In the chapters which follow you will learn about the tools and materials required for creating special paint finishes, and about the secrets of successful preparation. Read these sections carefully before embarking on your chosen project. Study the descriptions and photographs of the different techniques and finished projects, decide on any adaptations which will be necessary for your particular scheme or piece of furniture – and start painting!

Follow carefully the step-by-step instructions – and the details on finishing touches in Chapter 5 – to create a beautiful and professional-looking piece which will become a talking point in any room. Then, once you have gained in confidence and expertise, use the ideas in this book to help develop your very own designs for painted furniture – and a unique style for every room in your home.

2

TOOLS AND MATERIALS

You do not need a large armoury of specialist tools for the quick-and-easy approach to painting furniture, although there are some essentials you will require in order to carry out some of the techniques featured in the projects in this book.

BRUSH KIT

For applying primer, undercoat, paint, varnish and other liquids and sealants, a paintbrush is the essential basic tool. However, unless you have an ongoing enthusiasm for decorating – and have plenty of time for conscientious cleaning-up afterwards – you do not need to buy expensive types. A set of cheap, disposable, plastic-handled brushes, available from any do-it-yourself shop, will provide all the sizes of brush you will need to tackle most items of furniture featured in this book. Clean them afterwards if you like, but they are cheap enough to throw away when you have finished with them.

Typical sets contain a range of sizes, such as:
* 12mm (½in)– for painting fiddly, fairly inaccessible parts or fine details.
* 25mm (1in) – for painting narrow components, glazing bars and moulded panels.
* 50mm (2in) or 75mm (3in) – for general painting of surfaces.
* 100mm (4in) – for painting large, flat surfaces such as tabletops and panels.

IN SUSPENSION

If you have to break off while painting an item of furniture, or need to swap to another colour but don't want to waste time washing or cleaning, simply invest in a few sets of brushes.

Use the brush as necessary, then wrap it in transparent kitchen cling wrap and set aside; the paint will remain soft on the bristles for a few days, and you can simply unwrap it and use it again.

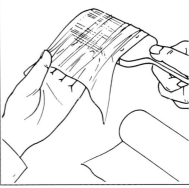

12mm (½in), 25mm (1in) and 50mm (2in) paintbrushes.

100mm (4in) paintbrush.

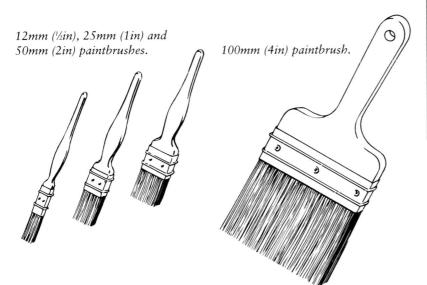

Dusting brush.

Soft Touch

A **dusting brush** is not essential for all painted techniques, but is vital for softening and spreading out glazes, as during marbling, and for stippling colour. A dusting brush has long, soft bristles set in a wooden handle, and is always used dry.

Dab hand

A **stencil brush** is a short, stubby brush with stiff bristles squared-off at the end. It is available in a range of sizes and is used to dab colour through the holes of a stencil, giving a clearer image than an ordinary paintbrush would allow. A 25mm (1in) size is adequate for most stencilling projects.

Fine lines

For marble veining, freehand painting and other detailed work, a set of fine, **artist's brushes**, available from artist's suppliers for painting in oils and watercolours, is a must. Choose a soft-bristled, sable-hair brush with a tapering point for painting fine motifs, veins and delicate features, and a blunt-ended hog's-hair brush for coarser details. A pencil-fine sable-hair brush is a useful addition for small-scale work.

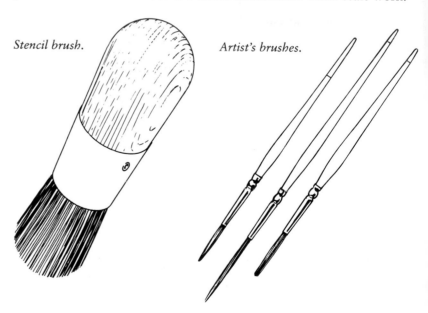

Stencil brush.   *Artist's brushes.*

ROLLERS

A **paint roller** is ideal for applying paint to large areas quickly – for example, when applying a basecoat to a large cabinet. There are basically two types, ranging in length from about 175mm (7in) to 330mm (13in), although smaller gloss rollers are available for painting narrow sections of woodwork. These are:

- Plastic foam – the cheapest option, and the one which gives the least acceptable finish, with tiny air bubbles left in the paint surface. The foam sleeves, which slot on to a cranked handle and are retained by a nut, can be disposed of after use.
- Roller sleeves – with a surface pile of synthetic fibre or sheepskin, which will give the best finish but are more costly. The sleeve fits on to a sprung wire cage on a cranked handle. Medium-pile types are the most useful; short-pile types are suitable for use with oil paints, while deep-pile versions are really only appropriate for heavily textured surfaces.

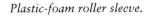

Medium-pile roller sleeve.

Plastic-foam roller sleeve.

Wire cage.

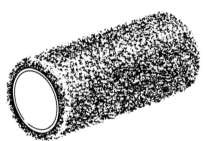

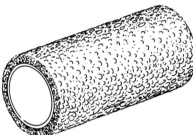

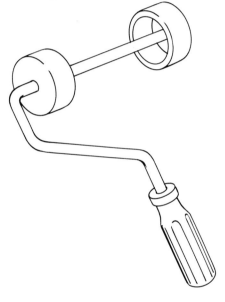

CLEANING SLEEVES

Unless you are using disposable foam rollers, you will need to wash out the sleeves after use, although you can store them overnight wrapped in kitchen cling wrap, as for brushes (see page 13).

To remove emulsion paint, get rid of the excess by rolling the roller back and forth on newspaper, and then rinse under a running hot tap. Work some washing-up liquid into the pile, massage, and then rinse out.

To remove oil paint, pour some white spirit into the roller tray and carefully roll the sleeve in the liquid, massaging the pile with your fingers. When the paint has dissolved, wash the sleeve thoroughly in a detergent solution of warm water, and then rinse in clean water.

Clean paint pads (see page 16) in the same way.

TRAY LINER

To save washing your roller or pad tray after use, line the base with aluminium cooking foil, folding it over the edges. When you have finished painting, decant any leftover paint into the can, then dispose of the foil cleanly.

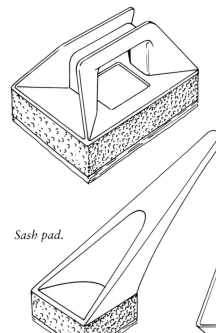

Tray tricks

A **roller tray** features a plastic or metal, sloping ribbed section and a deeper paint reservoir. To load the roller, dip the sleeve in the paint and roll it in the ribbed section to distribute the paint evenly.

Roller tray and roller.

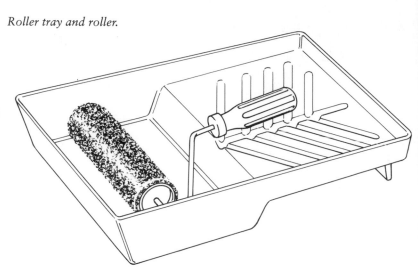

Standard paint pad.

PAINT PADS

For painting broad, flat areas, paint pads are supremely useful, and they can also be adapted to impress patterns on furniture, as shown on page 36. The rectangular pad consists of a plastic backing, with a foam strip stuck to it, topped with a short mohair pile; a handle slots into the backing. **Standard pads** measure about 75 × 180mm (3 × 7in), although small **sash pads** about 25mm (1in) square (intended for painting window glazing bars) are available. Pads are sold separately or in packs containing a special paint tray with a loading roller for paint distribution.

Paint-pad tray.

Sash pad.

The distressed finish, simple patterning and bright red painted highlights applied to the furniture in this understated scheme blend perfectly with the tones and design of an unusual antique picture.

SPECIAL EFFECTS

There are several handy tools which can be used to create special paint finishes.

Looks like grain

A nifty tool for creating wood-grain effects in wet glaze is a **rubber rocker**. About 100mm (4in) long, with a series of semi-circular ribs on its curved underside, the device is drawn through wet glaze and pivoted back and forth gradually to scoop up areas of the paint and leave an authentic-looking grain pattern (see page 52).

Rubber rocker.

Toothmarks

A flexible rubber **triangular comb** with three toothed edges can be drawn through wet glaze to leave the basecoat showing through in a series of lines. The tool can be used to produce vertical, horizontal, cross-hatched, diagonal, curving or random combed effects.

Spongy

A **natural sponge** can be used for applying mottled colour (see page 49) or dabbing glazes to create interesting textures. Choose a sponge that fits neatly into your hand and which has an evenly rounded face.

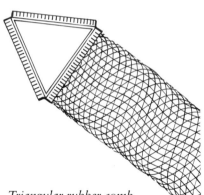

Triangular rubber comb.

SUNDRIES

In addition to the tools used for applying paint, you will need a few other items of equipment.

Good blades

You will need a sharp **craft knife or scalpel** and a set of replaceable blades for cutting stencils, making impression pads and general trimming.

For applying filler to defects in wooden furniture, use a flexible-bladed **filling knife.**

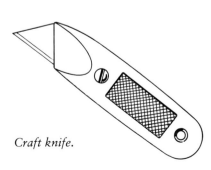

Craft knife.

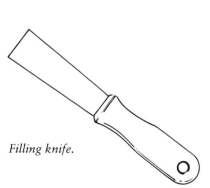

Filling knife.

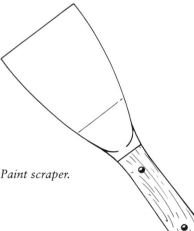

Paint scraper.

Finally, you will need a rigid-bladed **scraper**, for stripping off old paint finishes during preparation, and a **shavehook**, which has a triangular blade for stripping paint from mouldings – some types have a rounded blade to cope with deep mouldings.

Shavehook.

Rough treatment
You will need several sheets of **abrasive paper**, in coarse, medium and fine grades, for sanding down rough wood, smoothing previous paint finishes to form a key for the new treatment, and generally producing a fine, smooth finish between coats of paint or varnish.

Wire wool can be used as an alternative to abrasive paper for smoothing mouldings and carvings, and when removing old oil, wax or polished surfaces.

Masked off
Masking tape is available in rolls in various widths and is used, either on its own or in conjunction with sheets of paper, to mask off areas that you do not want painted. A good example would be when you are stencilling (see page 71).

Wipes and wads
Painting is messy at the best of times, so have to hand a pack of proprietary disposable **absorbent cloths** to cope with spills and catch drips and runs. **Lint-free cloths** should be used to apply glazes, polishes and varnishes.

PAINTS AND MATERIALS
There is such a vast selection of different paints on the market today that you may understandably be confused about which ones to use for special painted-furniture effects. However, if you keep speed and easy application in mind, the choice can be narrowed to just a few, which are listed below.

Emulsion paint
The most versatile of paints to use on painted furniture, emulsions are water-based, which means that they can be diluted with water. There is a huge range of colours from which to choose, and they can also be tinted using universal stainers (see page 20).

Oil-based paint
Most oil-based (sometimes known as alkyd) paints have either a highly gloss or a semi-gloss finish, described variously as satin, silk or eggshell. Based on a synthetic alkyd resin, they can be thinned with white spirit. Many colours are available, and they can also be tinted with universal stainers or artist's oil paints (see page 20).

Aerosol paint

Aerosol spray paints are a versatile means of applying paint to textured or uneven surfaces in order to create delicate blends and misty effects. Types for car-body retouching are fairly vividly coloured, while softer tones intended for home decorating are also available.

Artist's oil paint

Based on linseed oil to which pigments are added, artist's oil paints, available in tubes, can be used directly for fine work or to tint oil-based paints or glazes.

Poster paint

Available in powder form or ready-mixed in small containers or larger bottles, water-based poster paints can be used directly for fine work such as painting motifs or tinting emulsions. Widely used by children, the colour range is exciting and fresh.

Gouache and acrylics

Water-based paints, gouache and acrylics, available in tubes, can be used directly or to tint other water-based paints. Acrylics have a more vivid colour range than the more subdued gouache.

Universal stainers

Available in tubes or in special syringes, universal stainers are dyes which can be combined with emulsions or oil paints to create a unique colour.

Transparent oil glaze

Essential for paint effects which require a semi-transparent surface finish, such as marbling and dragging, this slow-drying glaze is readily available in cans. Diluted with white spirit, the opaque, creamy liquid can be coloured with artist's oil paints or universal stainers. It must be protected with varnish.

Metal paint

Oil-based metal paints, intended for protecting and colouring ironwork and other metal items, can be used on wooden furniture too. Spray paints have a smooth sheen, while canned versions may have a textured finish which resembles beaten metal. The colour range is somewhat limited.

White spirit

A clear solvent, white spirit is used for thinning oil-based paints and oil glazes and for cleaning brushes, rollers and other equipment used with them. It can also be used to create patterns on painted and glazed

Opposite: The light touch of the painted effects on chest and wardrobe in this young child's bedroom are a perfect complement to the rest of the decorative scheme. A narrow red highlight on the chest matches the edging on an unusual Lloyd-loom table, while the painted wardrobe panels depict favourite nursery-story scenes.

surfaces while still wet, for example the blurred blotches in marbling. It is available in plastic containers of various volumes, has a pronounced odour and should be used in a well-ventilated space.

Methylated spirit
Used to distress wet or dry emulsion, methylated spirit can be applied by sponge or flicked on by brush to create blotchy effects.

Varnish
Used to protect plain or painted surfaces, varnish provides a tough, clear film which can be either matt, semi-gloss or high gloss. Water-based and oil-based types are available, but polyurethane varnishes are easiest to use and very tough, although they do tend to yellow with age.

Spray-on glaze
As an alternative to varnish, clear glaze sold in aerosol form is invaluable for sealing water-based paint treatments to improve their wearability. This non-yellowing glaze, which contains the solvent acetone, must be used in a well-ventilated room. It is available in gloss or matt finish.

Wax polish and beeswax
Not only does polish give a subtle sheen to varnished, painted furniture or bare wood, but also, if scented with, say, lemon or lavender, can introduce a delightful aroma to your home. The wax is simply rubbed on with a soft, lint-free cloth, then buffed to a sheen with another soft cloth. Regular applications of wax will build up a pleasant patina on your furniture.

3

PREPARATION

Any decorative finishing you apply to your furniture will only be as good and long lasting as the time and effort you spent on preparation. Nothing will mar the finish more than surface imperfections (scars, dents, woodworm holes and so on), structural instability, an accumulation of dirt, dust and grease, or a build-up of previous paint finishes which obscure fine detail or create a poor base for the new treatment.

STRIPPING

Previously painted furniture need not be stripped back to bare wood if the finish is reasonably sound and not too heavily overpainted. Sanding off any glossy surface should leave a smooth base for applying the new finish, while emulsion-painted items can simply be sanded. However, if the existing paint is blistered or chipped, or if it was originally poorly applied, the only solution is to strip it back to bare wood. How you do this depends on several factors, such as the size of the item, how heavily overcoated it is, and whether it has any delicate moulded details.

Professional stripping

Large pieces of furniture can be dipped in a caustic bath and stripped to remove numerous paint films, although the treatment does raise the wood grain and leave it furry. Patient sanding down afterwards will restore the smooth finish.

Liquid or gel stripper

For stripping more intricate shapes, you can use a liquid or gel chemical stripper, although this method can be expensive for larger items.

These strippers are either water- or spirit-based, although there is no difference in the way they are used.

Paste stripper

An alternative method of stripping is to use a paste stripper, which is especially good for removing paint from delicate mouldings. Sold as a powder, it is mixed with water to a paste consistency, spread on and then peeled off, complete with the old paint. Work in a well-ventilated room, to avoid breathing in the fumes, and wear rubber gloves when applying the paste.

Liquid or gel stripper

  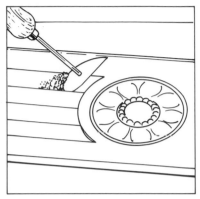

1 To apply the stripper, daub it liberally on to the painted surface using an old paintbrush and leave for about 10–15 minutes to allow the chemicals to soften and blister the surface.

2 Scrape off the softened paint with a scraping knife, then wash down the stripped wood using water or white spirit (depending on the type of stripper used) to neutralize the chemical action.

3 For moulded sections, use a shavehook, which has a shaped blade to reach into crevices and rounded sections. A wooden kebab skewer is ideal for picking softened paint from carvings.

Paste stripper

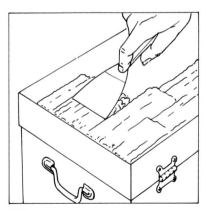 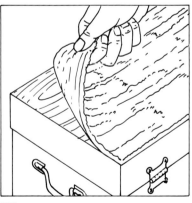

1 Trowel the paste on to the paintwork to a thickness of about 3mm (⅛in) and leave for about three hours to soften the paint film.

2 Carefully prise up a corner of the hardened paste and peel it off, complete with the old paint film. Wash the stripped wood and then sand.

A central floral motif has been painted on the door of a small wooden cupboard, picking up the tile design and adding a counterpoint to the geometric lines of wallcovering, skirting and dado, and furniture, in this bathroom decorated in brown tones.

Removing oil, wax and polish

Oil, wax or French polish finishes can be removed by rubbing gently with fine wire wool soaked in a solvent. For oil and wax, use white spirit to dissolve the finish; for French polish, use methylated spirit.

Wearing rubber gloves, gently rub along the wood grain with a wad of fine wire wool soaked in solvent. Rub with wire wool only around moulded components, such as the back of stick-back chairs.

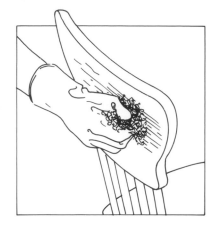

SANDING

It is essential to achieve a smooth surface for redecorating wooden furniture, and sanding with abrasives is the technique to use, after stripping off previous finishes, when a grain is raised or rough, and often between primer, undercoat and topcoats of paint. Abrasive papers consist of a paper backing coated with grains of crushed glass, garnet or carborundum. Use the correct grade: coarse grade is good for removing a heavy build-up of paint, but leaves a rough finish; medium grade is for general sanding, fine grade is for final smoothing.

Sanding by hand

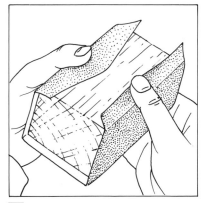

1 For sanding flat surfaces tear a strip from a sheet and wrap it around a wooden sanding block. Sand in the direction of the wood grain with long, smooth strokes.

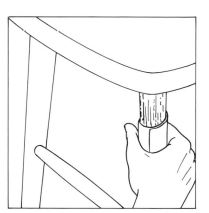

2 Abrasive paper rolled around a length of dowel is ideal for sanding moulded surfaces, while to sand, for example, a rounded leg simply wrap the strip around it and rub along the grain.

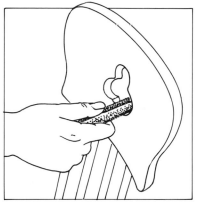

3 Intricate mouldings cannot be sanded successfully using abrasive paper, but a wad of wire wool – which also comes in medium and fine grades – will reach into crevices.

Machine sanding

An electric orbital sander is excellent for fine-sanding large, flat areas, such as the top of a chest or table.

KNOTTING

Knots in timber such as deal and pine can seep sticky resin for many years, and are likely to bleed through a subsequent paint finish, causing discoloration and blistering, unless sealed with a proprietary knotting liquid.

PRIMING

Bare wood, especially new wood, should be given a coat of primer, which prevents the subsequent coats of paint from being absorbed into the grain. Apply a liberal coat of primer to bare wood, brushing well into the wood grain, and allow to dry before overpainting. Priming is not necessary over sound paint finishes that have been rubbed down. There are various types of primer available, but an ordinary universal type will be suitable in most cases, except for highly resinous woods, where an aluminium primer should be used instead. An acrylic primer will also double as an undercoat.

FILLING

Cracks, splits, dents and coarse wood grain should be filled and sanded prior to the decorative treatment being applied, particularly for those techniques which require a perfectly smooth finish. Use a proprietary pre-mixed all-purpose filler, available in handy tubs and often with a spatula for application.

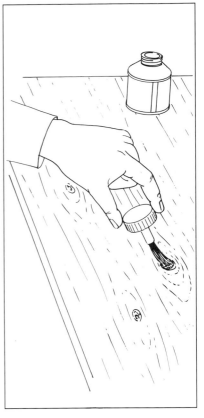

1 Brush (or dab on with a rag) the knotting liquid on to each resinous knot and leave to dry before priming.

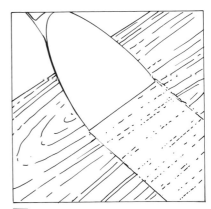

1 Spread the filler *across* the grain so that it fills the crack or other defect, then spread *along* the grain, allowing it to stand slightly proud of the surface. When the filler is hard, sand smooth.

UNDERCOATING

Undercoat is a type of highly pigmented paint which gives excellent coverage of wood and a good flat surface on which to apply an oil-based gloss or semi-gloss topcoat. (Emulsion requires no undercoat other than, in some cases, a diluted coat of the finish paint). Two coats may be needed to give the necessary depth of coverage. When dry, sand each undercoat. White undercoat is suitable under white gloss, but for darker colours a similar-coloured undercoat is necessary; many glosses have a specific undercoat sold for the purpose.

A stencilled pineapple design cleverly picks up the arrangement of glazing bars on the doors of this green-painted dresser. It is repeated across the top, together with a stylized leaf motif borrowed from the floor-covering design, to form a simple yet effective border.

the projects

The projects in this book have been carefully selected to cover a wide spectrum of painting techniques and decorative styles – there really is something for everyone!

All the effects are quick and easy to apply, but those classified as Simple Projects represent the most basic techniques, requiring no special skills or equipment other than everyday, readily available decorating tools and materials.

Once you have cut your decorative teeth on these, you will be able to tackle the paint techniques used in the Advanced Projects with confidence. Do not be put off by thinking that these projects must be hugely complex – most require only a basic kit of special but inexpensive tools, and the knack of applying the finishes is easy to learn.

spatter finish

A spattered paint finish is one of the easiest and quickest effects to produce – you simply flick a loaded paintbrush against a stick to create a shower of paint flecks across the surface. Yet spattering can create either a richly coloured, pronounced and durable texture or, in contrast, a mere hint of texture that does not obscure the base colour. Used to give a new lease of life to the outdated bedside cupboard in the opposite picture, spattering excels: successive applications of red, green and black dots flicked on to a background of rich blue mimics the tones of the tartan bedspread, pillows and lampshade in distinctly classical style. Applied more economically, in the picture below finer spatterings of colour on a pale background create a thoroughly modern effect on what is no more than a simple chipboard table, originally designed to be concealed beneath a cloth.

Above: A moderate spattering of mauve, blue and green on a pale blue tabletop contrasts starkly with the bold use of richer tones for wall, dado and floor, transforming a cheap round chipboard table into a stunningly modern focal point.

Spattered bedside cupboard
WOODEN BEDSIDE CUPBOARD
PAINT OR VARNISH STRIPPER
(IF NECESSARY)
SCRAPING KNIFE
WHITE SPIRIT
WIRE WOOL
MEDIUM- AND FINE-GRADE
ABRASIVE PAPER
NEWSPAPER
POLYTHENE DUST SHEET
OIL-BASED SEMI-GLOSS PAINT
(FOR BASECOAT)
MASKING TAPE
3 COLOURS OF OIL-BASED SEMI-
GLOSS PAINT (FOR SPATTERING)
25MM (1IN), 50MM (2IN) AND
75MM (3IN) PAINTBRUSHES
600MM (24IN) LENGTH OF
DOWEL WRAPPED WITH
ABSORBENT CLOTH

The surface of the cupboard should be basically sound, but previous coats of paint can be easily stripped off. Minor scratches will be concealed by the basecoat and subsequent spattered coats, but deep gouges and substantial woodworm damage will show through and mar the finish, which really looks best on a fairly smooth surface with fine lines.

You can apply a spattered finish to a veneered or melamine-faced cupboard, provided the thin veneer or coating is soundly fixed.

When choosing colours, you can select either a dark basecoat and fleck this with lighter colours, as in the tartan-toned bedside cupboard, or a light basecoat spattered finely with darker colours, as in the round table, where the spattered colours are those used to colour the legs of the table. The paint for spattering must be thinned with white spirit to such a consistency that it showers evenly from the brush: too thick and it will fly off in globules; too thin and it will run when it hits the surface. The only way to achieve the correct consistency is to experiment and practise on newspaper.

The intensity of the final effect depends on the colour you have chosen for the basecoat, the number and colours of the spattered coats, and the depth of coverage of the tiny dots. By using larger or smaller brushes you can control the heaviness or sparsity of paint flecks on the basecoat, but you should avoid too great a build-up of spattered paint, as this will create areas of solid colour that would spoil the effect and cause it to look patchy.

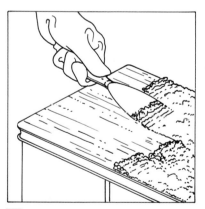

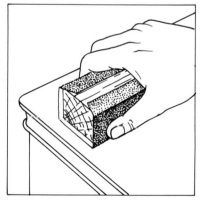

1 Remove any knobs, catches or other items you do not want spattered. Prepare the surface of the cupboard by stripping off any previous paint or varnish finish using a proprietary liquid, gel or paste stripper (see page 23). Remember to wear rubber gloves.

2 Remove the paint finish with a metal scraping knife (with a paste stripper, the substance can be peeled off, complete with the paint finish). Wipe the surface with white spirit to remove traces of the stripper. If the cupboard has mouldings, rub these with wire wool soaked in paint stripper.

3 Sand the cupboard with medium-followed by fine-grade abrasive paper wrapped around a block of wood, to produce a smooth surface.

4 Wipe over with white spirit again to remove grease and dust. Stand the cupboard, and any removable drawers, on sheets of newspaper ready for painting. When you come to spatter, cover a wide area of floor with a polythene dust sheet to catch the inevitable stray flecks of paint.

5 Paint the entire cupboard with undercoat and allow to dry thoroughly. Next, apply your chosen basecoat using a 75mm (3in) paintbrush, and allow to dry thoroughly. If the basecoat is light in colour, you may have to apply a second coat once the first has dried.

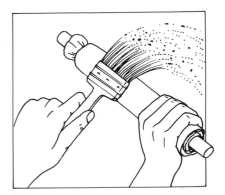

6 Mask off any surfaces you do not want to spatter, such as the sides or insides of drawers, using newspaper and masking tape. To prepare your spattering equipment, wrap a disposable absorbent cloth around the length of dowel, securing with string or freezer-bag ties, to absorb the 'shock' caused by the brush hitting the dowel. Load a 50mm (2in) brush with the first spatter colour and, aiming it at a sheet of newspaper, flick off excess paint.

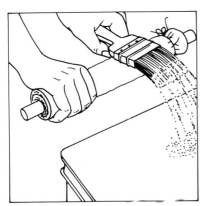

7 To apply the first spattering, hold the brush parallel to the surface and hit the ferrule (metal band) of the brush against the padded stick. The paint will rain from the brush in a series of tiny dots, spattering the base colour. Continue spattering until you have an even coverage of dots over all surfaces.

8 While the first spattered colour is drying, clean the brush in white spirit and shake dry. Brush back and forth on newspaper to remove excess solvent and to check that none of the first colour remains. To apply the second spattered colour, repeat step 7, aiming for a coverage that does not obscure the first coat.

9 To avoid too great a build-up of colour, it is best to use a 25mm (1in) paintbrush to spatter a third colour on to the cupboard: this will give a looser distribution of paint flecks, which adds accent to the other tones rather than creating a more defined coverage.

impressed patterns

Repeating simple geometric patterns on a plain background gives a fascinating textured effect that can enhance many items of furniture, such as the plain, matt-black-painted tea trolley daubed with a checkerboard of yellow squares shown in the picture opposite, or the dainty pink trunk dotted randomly with jaunty triangles in the picture below. You can use many existing items for impressing patterns – fruit and vegetables for instance – but cutting your own printing blocks from foam paint pads enables you to create the shapes you want. The technique is simplicity itself to apply – just dab the pile of the cut-down pad into ordinary emulsion or semi-gloss paint and press it on to the prepared surface. Impressing patterns can create either a bold and graphic effect or a pretty, delicate treatment: press heavily for a blurred effect or lightly for fainter, blotchy finish.

Above: A pretty treasure trunk for a young girl's bedroom, which picks out
the delicate pink in the floral curtains and the roses outside the window
for the basecoat, and to finish, is decorated with a random scattering
of deeper pink triangles.

Geometric tea trolley
WOODEN TEA TROLLEY
EMULSION PAINT OR OIL-BASED
BLACKBOARD PAINT (FOR
BASECOAT)
EMULSION PAINT OR OIL-BASED
SEMI-GLOSS (FOR IMPRESSING)
CLEAR MATT SPRAY-ON GLAZE OR
MATT VARNISH
(IF USING EMULSION PAINT)
PAINT PAD, HANDLE AND TRAY
SCALPEL OR CRAFT KNIFE

The first thing to do is to ensure that the surface to be painted is basically sound and free from grease and dirt. Strip off any previous paint or varnish finishes and sand smooth. The effect looks best when matt paint is used – the sheen of high gloss tends to detract from the delicate nature of the impressed patterns, although you can use an eggshell semi-gloss. Choose either two very different colours, such as the black and yellow of the trolley, or different tones of the same colour, such as the pale and dark pinks of the trunk. You could impress more colours for a more complex design, but the effect has a primitive simplicity that suits minimal colour changes.

The size of the shape you choose to impress is limited by the size of the paint pad; pads sold for home decorating come in a range of sizes, from a small 25mm (1in) square to a larger rectangle measuring 75mm × 180mm (3 × 7in). For smaller patterns, use a smaller pad cut with one shape only; for larger or repeat patterns you can – as with the trolley's checkerboard – cut two or more patterns from a single pad and impress several together. The checkerboard was produced using a 75 × 180mm (3 × 7in) pad cut into two squares with a 30mm (1¼in) gap between; in this way, only eight impressions were needed to complete the sixteen-square tabletop.

1 Paint the surface with the basecoat and allow to dry thoroughly. It is a good idea to use the colour you plan to impress on the basecoat to accent the effect – here, the yellow has been used for the lower shelf of the trolley. You could even reverse the effect by impressing black squares on this shelf.

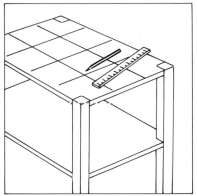

2 Work out the overall pattern you intend to impress and draw faint pencil guidelines to help you when positioning the paint pad. The patterning does not need to be precise, but should be basically symmetrical when it is viewed overall.

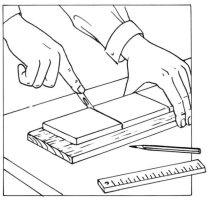

3 With the pad removed from its slide-on handle, mark the pattern you want to cut on the pile face, using a felt-tipped pen. Avoid complex shapes; they are difficult to cut and will blur on printing. Place the pad, pile uppermost, on a cutting board and use a scalpel or craft knife to slice through the pile and the foam beneath to cut out the shape. Do *not* cut through the pad's backing.

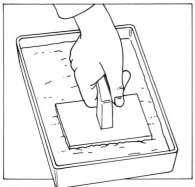

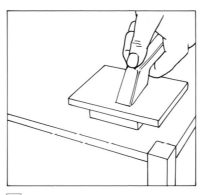

4 Replace the pad handle. Pour a little emulsion or semi-gloss paint into the paint tray – not too much, for this effect is very economical on paint – and dab the paint pad evenly into it. Do nor overload the pad or the impression will be too thick and blurred. If you get too much paint on the pile, scrape off the excess against the rim of the tray.

5 Position the pad squarely over the surface to be impressed, aligned with your pencil guides if necessary, then press down. Make sure the pad touches the surface as squarely as possible and do not move it sideways or the impression will be smudged. Lift off the pad cleanly to leave the impression.

6 Move the pad, without reloading it with more paint, to the next position and make the second impression. If the image is starting to get fainter, reload the pad with more paint. Allow the paint to dry.

7 If you have used emulsion paint you will need to seal the finish or subsequent spills will stain and mark the effect. Use a clear matt spray-on glaze or apply several coats of matt polyurethane varnish.

spray painting

Spray paints produce a soft delicate mist that enables you to create fine blends and tones of colour, and are ideally suited to painting complex textures such as wicker, cane and the finer strands of Lloyd loom, which would clog up with paint applied by brush. Used in conjunction with simple masking, you can form patterns or motifs: either subtle, as with the shoal of tiny fishes swimming merrily across the dainty Lloyd-loom chair in the picture opposite, or more defined and dominant. The nautical nature of the chair is accentuated by the accessories surrounding it – starfish and shells – and by the rich Mediterranean colours used: a pale sky blue resembling frothy surf over a deeper sea blue. Aerosol car paints are the best choice because of the huge range of colours available and their durability.

Above: This wicker laundry basket has been spray-painted white, masked to create bright yellow edging that fades away gently, and encircled by a pair of vivid blue bands.

Spray-painted Lloyd-loom chair
LLOYD-LOOM CHAIR
POLYTHENE DUST SHEET
SPRAY PAINT IN CHOSEN COLOURS
TRACING PAPER
MASKING TAPE
HARDBOARD OR
PLASTIC LAMINATE
(USED AS CUTTING BOARD)
SCALPEL

For this project, the Lloyd-loom chair itself should be in as good condition as possible – you can easily pick up fine specimens from junk shops and antique shops at bargain prices. Try to obtain one which hasn't been overpainted with gloss, as many unfortunately were, because this is virtually impossible to remove without damaging the loom itself. This basically consists of fine paper wrapped around wire, which is subsequently woven; consequently, any chemical strippers or excessive scraping will ruin the loom. If you cannot find a suitable Lloyd-loom chair, a cheaper wicker type will do.

The complexity of the fishy design on this chair belies its straightforward application: the chair is sprayed in the darker tone of blue, allowed to dry, and then oversprayed with a fine mist of lighter blue. The fish are formed by masking-tape cut-outs stuck to the first coat and then removed after the second coat has been applied, leaving their vivid shaped picked out in the original colour.

Work in a well-ventilated room or, preferably, outside on a calm, dry, windless day. Surround the chair with a large polythene dust sheet to catch the inevitable overspill of paint – to create the misty effect you will have to move the aerosol can rapidly back and forth. For this reason, wear a facemask and old clothes.

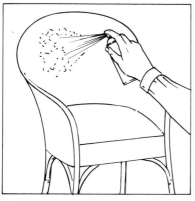

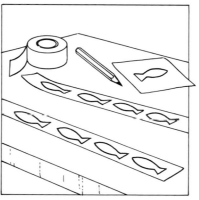

1 Stand the chair on a large dustsheet. Shake the can of basecoat thoroughly to mix the paint, and then apply with the can held vertically about 600mm (24in) from the surface. Work slowly and consistently so that the basecoat covers the original surface well. Do not hold the can too close to the chair or the paint will be applied too thickly and may run.

2 Trace the shape of the fish from the actual-size template given below and transfer to the masking tape, stuck temporarily to the shiny side of a sheet of hardboard or offcut of plastic laminate used as a cutting board.

3 Cut carefully around the outline of the fishes with a sharp scalpel, but leave them stuck to the cutting board until they are needed.

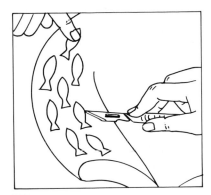 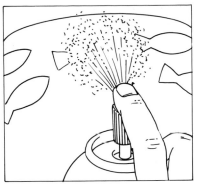 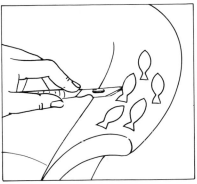

4 Peel each fish shape in turn from the cutting board and stick to the chair. Run a wavy line of fish, nose-to-tail, across the base of the seat, then place another line around the curved back of the chair.

5 Using the topcoat paint spray, with extravagant sweeps, apply a fine mist over the entire chair, but concentrate the colour over the masked-off fish.

6 When the topcoat is nearly dry, peel off each fish mask in turn, using the blade of the scalpel to lift the tape. The shape of the fish will appear in the basecoat, accentuated by the topcoat, which should fade gently to the base colour elsewhere on the chair.

The template given here is 240% of the smaller pattern for making masking-tape masks for the fish motifs. For larger fish, use the squares of the diagram on the right to scale up the motif. Use broader masking tape for larger fish.

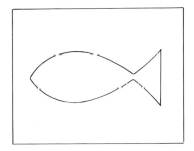 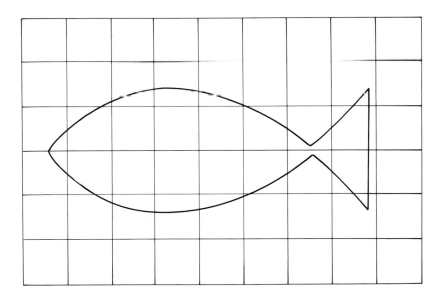

metallized finish

Glistening beaten metal adds a high-tech sparkle to everyday objects, but real metal furniture is costly, heavy and prone to rust. Why not simply 'metallize' an inexpensive piece of wooden furniture? Spray-on or paint-on metal paints are intended for protecting existing metalwork – railings, gates and other ironmongery – from the effects of corrosion, but they are also ideal for applying to wood, giving it a durable long-lasting all-weather finish or a tough, chip-resistant coating, as with the chipboard melamine-faced shelf unit in the picture opposite, which is to hold books in a child's room. Modern metal paints are available in a range of attractive colours, such as red, green, blue and yellow, in addition to the usual black, bronze and silver, so the furniture need not be utilitarian – the shelf carcass, for example, is thickly coated with a deep red hammer finish, while green metal paint picks out the shelf edging. Little preparation of surfaces is needed, provided they are reasonably sound and free from dust and grease: the thick paint will cope with minor cracks and dents, filling and binding them.

Above: The hammered-metal finish on this common-or-garden deckchair and matching drinks table reflects the pool water wonderfully and catches the sunlight. Modern metal paints can even be colour co-ordinated to your choice of deckchair fabric.

MATERIALS

Metallized bookshelves
SHELF UNIT
MEDIUM-GRADE ABRASIVE PAPER
AND WOOD BLOCK
WHITE SPIRIT
MASKING TAPE
SHARP TRIMMING KNIFE
HAMMER-FINISH METAL PAINT
DISPOSABLE PAINTBRUSHES

Metal paints have a powerful odour, so it is essential to work in a well-ventilated room – open the doors and windows – or, preferably, outside. You may find it beneficial to wear a disposable facemask to protect your lungs from the fumes. Certainly you should wear rubber gloves when using the paint, as it is notoriously difficult to wash off the skin. Mix up the paint thoroughly and apply thickly with a disposable paintbrush; do not attempt to wash out and reuse brushes, as metal paint is not kind to them.

When applying the paint, coat the surface liberally with a well-loaded brush, allowing the paint to flow to its own level. For this reason it is best to paint only horizontal surfaces, allowing each to dry before turning the shelf unit to present another horizontal surface. The paint goes on flat, but soon assumes a hammered appearance as it settles. If you apply too thin a coat and the wood finish glares through, it is best to wait until the paint is touch-dry before applying another, more liberal coat on top.

Metal paint such as this may appear dry to the touch, but it actually takes some hours to set fully hard. Avoid placing any objects on the shelves for at least two days, particularly if you have applied successive or very thick coats of paint, or you could find they sink into the surface and cause an ugly ridge. Once set fully, however, the paint finish is eminently tough and knock-resistant, lasting many years before repainting is necessary.

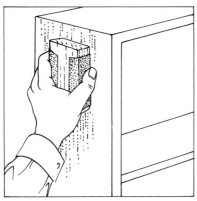

1 Sand the entire unit with medium-grade abrasive paper wrapped around a block of wood, and then brush off the dust. Even if the shelf unit is laminated or melamine faced, sanding will abrade the surface enough to aid adhesion of the metal paint, although it will stick successfully to quite shiny surfaces, as it is intended for application to metal.

2 Wipe over all surfaces with white spirit to remove any grease or dirt, and then allow to dry.

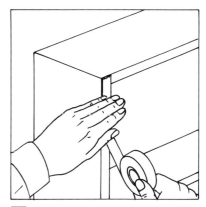

3 If you are applying a two-tone finish, mask off the edges of the shelf and around the perimeter of the carcass with masking tape to avoid runs of one colour affecting the other. Once applied, trim it to the thickness of the wood using a sharp trimming knife.

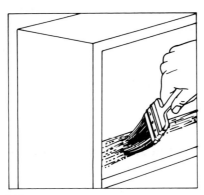

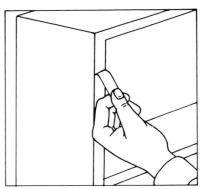

4 Mix the paint thoroughly and then apply with a well-loaded brush in broad, even strokes. Avoid overbrushing, as this will cause the paint to drag, pull out bristles and give patchy coverage. If this does happen, leave the paint until touch-dry and then apply a second coat.

5 Continue to paint the shelves and the carcass back, allowing the paint to flow to its own level. The hammered finish will appear once the paint has settled.

6 Once the paint has started to dry, peel off the masking tape. Do not leave it until the paint has become touch-dry, or you could peel it off at the edges. Use a narrower brush to apply the second colour to the edges of the shelves, taking care not to get any on the shelf surface.

OPTIONAL EFFECT

For a sleek shiny metallized finish, use smooth metal paint, which is best applied by aerosol spray. It is available in the same range of colours as hammer finish and provides just as durable a coating.

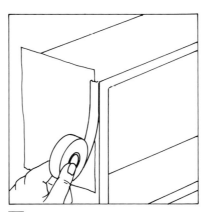

1 Mask off areas not to be painted in one colour, such as the shelf edges, and then spray evenly, moving the aerosol back and forth until good coverage is achieved. Avoid overspraying, as this will result in runs forming on vertical surfaces.

2 Peel off the masking tape and allow the paint to dry thoroughly before masking it off with paper and tape to leave the unpainted shelf edges visible. Spray again in the second colour, then remove the mask and allow the paint to dry.

sponging and sponge-stencilling

Create a nautical effect in a sunny bathroom with a jolly sponge-painted bath panel that reflects the allure of sea spray and sand (as shown opposite). Adorn it with sponge-stencilled starfish and shells, and accessorize with seaside mementoes to set a very positive style for the room. Sponging is an ideal method for colouring flat areas, particularly on manmade boards – depending on the build-up of colour you apply, it produces either a soft mottled effect or a deeper texture, which nevertheless only partially conceals the base colour. Stencilling with a sponge enables you to create softer, more blended motifs than is possible with brush-stencilling, and if you use children's poster paints you will discover a much more exciting colour range than the often bland emulsions. Provided you seal the surface, the bath panels will withstand any amount of bathtime frolics!

Above: Pretty sponge-stencilled ivy leaves in tones of green, linked by fine
fronds, curl around the legs of a petite plant stand, delicately coloured in
minty green and softened with a mist of sponged leafy green.

MATERIALS

Sponged bath panel

BATH PANEL WITH CENTRAL
FRAME
WHITE AND SEA-BLUE EMULSION
PAINT
CHILDREN'S POSTER PAINT IN
BRIGHT BLUE, DARK BLUE,
YELLOW AND ORANGE
PLASTIC CONTAINERS
(FOR HOLDING PAINT)
NATURAL SPONGE
25MM (1IN) AND 65MM (2½IN)
PAINTBRUSHES
FINE, ARTIST'S PAINTBRUSH
PIECE OF CARD
TRACING PAPER
CLEAR FILM (FOR STENCILS)
SCALPEL
SPRAY-ON MATT GLAZE OR CLEAR
MATT POLYURETHANE VARNISH

In order to paint the bath panel successfully, it is best to remove it from the framework to which it is attached, usually with screws, and lay each section on a flat surface. If the panel is plain, pin lengths of moulding to the surface, mitring the corners for neatness, to create false panels.

There are two secrets to successful sponging: using a sponge with the right texture and starting off subtly. If you proceed gently to begin with, you can always increase the amount of colour or texture and fill in sparse areas.

The motifs – shell, starfish, and an additional seahorse motif you may wish to incorporate – are given on page 90. Trace these shapes and use an enlarging and reducing photocopier to make them the size you require. Transfer the motifs to clear film and cut out using a scalpel – the film allows you to see the areas surrounding the motif, making positioning much easier than with standard stencil paper.

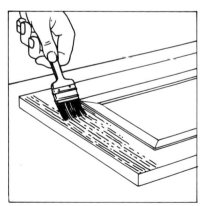

1 Paint the bath-panel sections with as many coats of white emulsion as it takes to give a flat, even basecoat for the sponging. You can use a roller for speed, but you will have to fit the mouldings afterwards and paint these with a brush.

2 Dip the sponge into the bright blue poster paint and sponge around the outer edge of each section, holding a piece of card vertically to form an edge to paint up to. Once the first sponging has dried, sponge again to give the depth of colour you require.

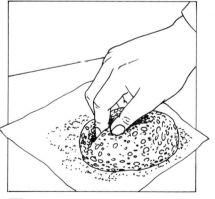

3 You need to use a gentle dabbing motion when sponging and, after each application, it is useful to dab off excess paint from the face of the sponge on to a piece of scrap paper or wood, so that the end result is consistent.

4 Draw a faint pencil line to mark the curve of the sand and sea on the central section and sponge above this with sea-blue emulsion and below with yellow poster paint. Wash the sponge between changing colours so that each colour remains pure.

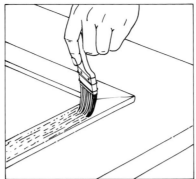

5 When the sponged areas are dry, use a 25mm (1in) paintbrush to paint the raised mouldings in sea-blue emulsion and then leave to dry prior to stencilling.

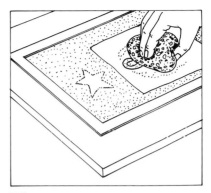

6 Position each stencil on the sections as required and sponge on white emulsion, using an offcut of sponge, to create a white mask on the background, so that the image stands out crisply from the base. Leave each motif to dry before painting the one next to it.

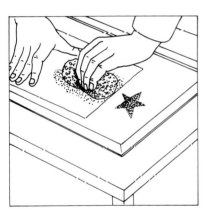

7 Place the stencil back over the white mask and fill in with the appropriate colour – dark blue for the starfish, orange and yellow for the shells – dabbing the colour on gently and making sure you hold the stencil absolutely still.

8 The sea shells should be sponged in a two-tone effect: orange first, and then yellow in the centre, gently fading away to give a three-dimensional effect. Make sure the orange is perfectly dry before sponging on the yellow or the colours will smudge.

9 Add subtle accents to the starfish motif by dabbing on darker blue along each of its arms, using a fine, artist's paintbrush. Once the painting is complete, seal it thoroughly with two or three coats of spray-on matt glaze or clear matt polyurethane varnish – in such close proximity to water, the emulsion and poster paints would soon run and spot.

graining

Imitating the natural grain of attractive wood is an art in itself and was, in the past, used to invest cheaper grades of timber with a richer appearance. You do not have to be a skilled craftsman, however, to produce convincing grain effects using a simple, cheap device known as a 'rocker'. With this you can apply pinelike grain patterns to the plainest of woods, or even to manmade boards, such as melamine-faced chipboard, as demonstrated with the handsome drinks cabinet shown in the picture opposite, which is nothing more than a budget self-assembly unit. For a realistic-looking wood grain, choose only natural colours over a wood-coloured background; for a more flamboyant grainy effect, however, you can use colours which resemble limed or bleached wood, or the blue-on-yellow scheme adopted for the cabinet.

Above: A rustic-style kitchen chair with pronounced woody grain, created with a buttermilk basecoat overpainted with caramel-brown and grained using a rocker.

MATERIALS
Grained drinks cabinet
SELF-ASSEMBLY CABINET
MEDIUM-GRADE ABRASIVE PAPER
OIL-BASED SEMI-GLOSS PAINT
(BASE AND GRAINING COATS)
RUBBER ROCKER
WHITE SPIRIT AND CLOTH
DUSTING BRUSH
PAINT PAD OR ROLLER AND TRAY
25MM (1IN) PAINTBRUSH
GLOSS OR SEMI-GLOSS CLEAR
OIL-BASED VARNISH

The cabinet needs little preparation other than sanding down to key the shiny melamine to accept the basecoat. You can apply the basecoat using a brush, but because the graining is best done over as smooth a surface as possible, a paint pad or roller excels; you will, however, need a small brush to paint in the edges where the roller cannot reach. If you need to apply a second basecoat, do this when the first is sufficiently dry, after about two hours.

When the basecoat is thoroughly dry, you can apply the graining coat. It is best to use an oil-based paint thinned by about 20 per cent with white spirit. Experiment with the mixture first on a spare piece of board – if the glaze is too thin, the grain pattern will run; if too thick, the pattern will smudge and blur.

The tool used to create the grain pattern is a rubber pad, the surface of which is ribbed with a series of semi-circles. When drawn through the wet glaze and rocked gently back and forth, the ribbing scoops up the paint, leaving areas of the basecoat showing through a realistic wood-grain effect. To soften a dominant grain pattern and blend it in with the basecoat, a dry dusting brush can be drawn lightly over the surface.

Once dry, the grained finish can be given a coat of oil-based clear varnish, both to enhance the effect and to protect the finish from knocks and spills.

1 Remove the knobs and other fittings from the cabinet so that the grain pattern will be consistent. For a unified look, you can paint the fittings in the colour used to grain the cabinet. Sand down the cabinet with medium-grade abrasive paper, and then wipe over with white spirit. When dry, apply a coat of your base colour, using a paint roller or pad for the flattest finish. Apply a second basecoat if necessary.

2 Dilute the graining colour with white spirit and test its consistency on a piece of board before working on the actual cabinet. When you are satisfied with the consistency, apply a thin coat by brush to an easily manageable section of the unit – you will need to work quickly to avoid the glaze drying out, so do not apply more paint than you can grain easily in one go.

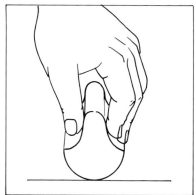

3 Hold the rocker between fingers and thumb and place its rounded surface on the wet glaze. If you are graining a vertical surface, work from the top down; for a horizontal surface, draw the rocker towards you.

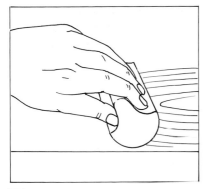 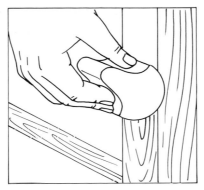 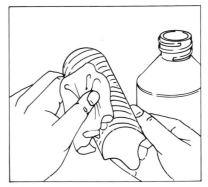

4 As you pull the rocker along, gradually alter the angle at which you hold it so that its ribbing collects the wet glaze and forms a unique but realistic wood grain pattern, with the basecoat showing through. Take care not to jerk the rocker or you will smudge the grain pattern.

5 Graining the narrow edges of the cabinet, or the edges of the doors, calls for more care, as it is easy for the rocker to slip and mar the pattern. Work slowly, without altering the angle of the rocker as much as you would on a flatter surface.

6 After each pass wipe the rocker on a cloth soaked in white spirit, so that excess paint is removed from the ribbing, making for cleaner, crisper grain patterning. If the rocker becomes too clogged, rinse it in a container of white spirit, dry off and then reuse.

 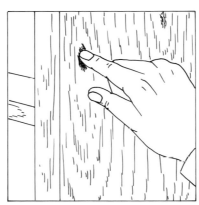 

7 If you are happy with the fairly vivid effect of the grain as it is, simply leave it to dry. For a softer, more subtle effect, use a dusting brush to blend in the graining with the base colour; this will also remove any deposits of glaze left behind by the rocker. Flick the brush lightly along the 'grain' direction.

8 Add realistic-looking 'knots' to the grained effect by dabbing a finger in the glaze and pressing it on to the surface, smudging it slightly.

9 When the graining is dry, apply a coat of oil-based clear varnish in gloss or semi-gloss finish. If you wish, you can then buff the surface with wax polish for an intense sheen. Replace the knobs, handles and other fittings.

primitive freehand

There is an innocent appeal in furniture that has been adorned with simple, almost childlike, motifs rendered by a hand unskilled in art – in cultures across the world, for generations, ordinary people have decorated their homes and their possessions with symbols that suggest their ethnic origins. The corner display cupboard in the picture opposite, for example, has a distinctly Romany appearance, using the rich reds, greens and blues that are inherent in many Mediterranean countries. You do not require any artistic aptitude to create a similar effect – just a basic appreciation of the use of colour and the decorative placement of motifs and other embellishments.

Above: Primitively painted leaves, stems and berries hang in garlands around a country-style plate rack painted in a rich creamy gloss, while a streaky red line picks out the moulded, curved front edge.

Hand-painted corner cupboard
CORNER DISPLAY CUPBOARD OR
OTHER UNIT
PAINT STRIPPER
MEDIUM- AND FINE-GRADE
ABRASIVE PAPER
MATT EMULSION IN RED, YELLOW,
SLATE-GREY AND GREEN
75MM (3IN) PAINTBRUSH
(FOR CUPBOARD)
FINE, ARTIST'S PAINTBRUSHES
(FOR MOTIFS)

For this project, choose a piece of furniture which contains some decorative features – mouldings, finials, areas of fretwork – which will help in the positioning of motifs and placement of colours. The corner unit shown here, for instance, has a wavy-edged moulding at the top with a fretwork arrangement of pillars, which can be considered as separate elements when deciding on colours. Avoid overly complicated colour schemes, however, or the end result will be merely chaotic; a minimalist treatment is far more effective. The simple zig-zag lines, painted in green and complementary red and running along the top of the unit, contrast perfectly with the wavy top edge, which is painted yellow, while the two plain side panels are the ideal ground for a symbolic representation of flowers on a stem, rendered as fine curving lines and red triangles on a yellow background.

Sketch out your ideas on paper first, to help you define and refine your choice of symbols, looking through magazines and books as a source of colours and motifs. To depict flowers, for example, simply reduce them to their basic geometric shapes; for a softer, less, symbolic effect, sketchy representations of the various elements will suffice, as in the country-style plate-rack on page 56.

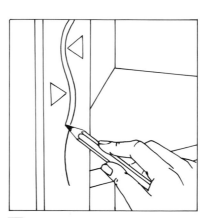

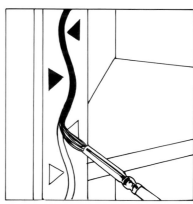

1 Strip off any previous paint finishes and sand the unit. Paint the insides of the unit first, choosing the deeper colours. Paint the front face and any decorative feature, such as the wavy edge at the top and bottom on this corner unit, in the lighter colour.

2 Pencil in your motifs faintly on the face of the unit before applying even the basecoat of paint, erasing and adapting them as necessary. Once perfected, overpainting – provided the colour is pale – should allow their faint image to show through as a guide.

3 Using fine, artist's brushes, paint the symbolic flower stems and blooms, working from the top down so that you do not smudge newly painted parts.

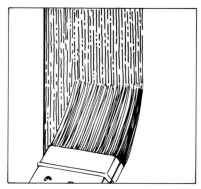

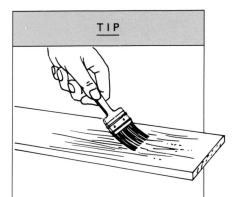

4 Mix up a glaze of green semi-gloss paint and white spirit and, after testing the consistency, apply it to the cabinet. When painting the doors, run the brush down one of the outer verticals.

5 Immediately take the dry dragging brush and draw it smoothly down the wet glaze, with the bristles fairly flat to the surface. Press sufficiently hard so that the glaze is removed streakily but evenly, allowing the buttermilk basecoat to shine through. If you remove too much glaze, wipe it all off with white spirit and start again.

TIP

Test the consistency of the glaze on an offcut of wood before applying it to the cabinet.

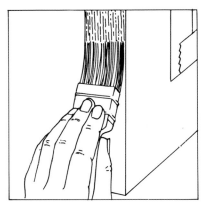

6 Where the horizontal rails of the door meet the verticals, use a piece of card as a shield to prevent streaking the vertical dragging when applying glaze to the top and bottom rails.

7 Glaze and drag the opening edge of the cabinet door, and the top and underside of the horizontals, but do not bother glazing the hinged edge of the door, as it will not be visible.

marbling

The coolness of marble adds a refreshing tone to a decorative scheme – but the real thing is costly and often impractical. Painted simulations of its subtle surface nuances, intricate veining and myriad colours need not be the slow skilled technique it is often considered to be. Provided you accept a finish that is more of an approximation to marble than an authentic copy, you can invest an item of furniture with a surface that has sumptuous texture and softly blurred colouring, such as the distinctive wooden coffee table in the picture opposite – a style that is readily available from pine stockists. The thick tabletop, with its rounded edges and corners, is set on stout legs painted matt black to resemble heavy slate and offset the pale creams, pinks and yellows of the 'marble' finish.

Above: Built-in alcove bookshelves have been given a finish that simulates the marble of the adjacent fireplace – an elegant treatment for a utilitarian feature.

Marble coffee table
WOODEN COFFEE TABLE
DUST SHEET
BLACKBOARD PAINT
WHITE EGGSHELL PAINT
2 50MM (2IN) PAINTBRUSHES
TRANSPARENT OIL GLAZE
WHITE SPIRIT
LINT-FREE CLOTH
ARTIST'S PAINTBRUSH
ARTIST'S OIL PAINTS
DUSTING BRUSH
VEINING FEATHER
MATT OR SEMI-GLOSS
POLYURETHANE VARNISH
WAX POLISH

The legs and rails of this coffee table are painted with matt black blackboard paint. You may need to apply two or more coats for best coverage and density.

Two or more coats of smooth white eggshell paint will provide an ideal base for the 'marble' finish. The process consists of applying a film of transparent oil glaze to the basecoat; then, in this slow-drying medium – it can take three or four days to dry – you can draw in fidgety, blurred veins in artist's oils, meandering diagonally across the surface, as in real marble. Soften the veins by stroking with a soft long-bristled dusting brush or stippling to break up the colour. Then add more veins in a lighter colour and soften them too, so that the overall surface assumes a hazy blur.

Different types of marble can be suggested by tinting the oil glaze with colours such as green, blue and yellow, or by spattering solvent on to the wet glaze to produce puddles which separate the colour. Sponging the surface can also produce interesting textures in the wet glaze.

Oil glaze itself does not wear well and so you will need to give the finish two or three coats of matt or semi-gloss varnish to protect it. Waxing the surface will create a sheen which can enhance the effect of the marbling.

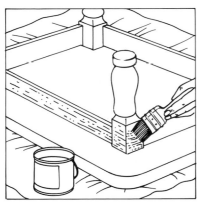

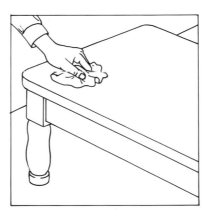

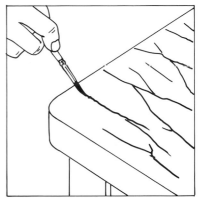

1 Prepare the table for repainting, and then paint the legs and rails with blackboard paint. If the table is likely to be positioned in an exposed place, give it a coat of matt varnish, as blackboard paint tends to scuff easily. Apply two or more coats of white eggshell paint to the tabletop.

2 Dilute one part transparent oil glaze with one part white spirit and apply a thin coating to the tabletop. Use a lint-free cloth rather than a brush, which would not give a smooth enough film. It is essential to work in a draught-free area, as the glaze easily collects dust, which could mar the finish.

3 Using a fine, artist's paintbrush and black, artist's oil paint, form the larger, more dominant veins in the wet glaze. Draw the brush in a jerky movement to create veins running diagonally across the 'slab'. Add occasional dabs and splatters of paint to create the finer surface details.

[4] Now use the tips of a dry soft-bristled dusting brush to stroke the veins very carefully in all directions, softening their outlines. Be careful not to spread the veins out too much and always end with brushstrokes along their length so they still have a definite line of direction.

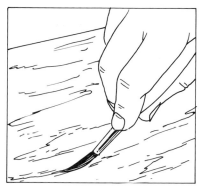

[5] Draw in finer veins in another artist's oil colour, such as the peachy tone used on the coffee table, using a smaller brush. Add some highlights of white, artist's oil paint, running alongside the black veins. Soften the peachy veins and highlights with the dusting brush.

[6] Dip a feather in the oil glaze and push it, against the lie of the feather, jerkily through the surface glaze, avoiding the veined areas, to create blurred streaks that help to give an impression of depth and translucency. Draw in the odd 'pebble' shape with white paint and soften the effect using the dusting brush.

OPTIONS

There are various other techniques you can use to suggest different types of marble. Experiment with yellow, green or brown glazes and add some of the features below.

[7] Leave the table somewhere well ventilated but dust free so that the oil glaze can dry properly. This may take up to four days, during which time the 'marble' surface will be delicate and easily marked. Once dry, coat it with matt or semi-gloss polyurethane varnish, and wax for a sheen.

[1] Create mottled patches in the wet glaze by dabbing the surface with a natural sponge which has been soaked in white spirit. You will need to dab at the perimeter of the mottled area with a dry cloth to prevent the glaze spreading further.

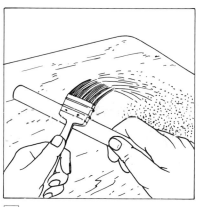

[2] Spatter white spirit from a brush on to the wet glaze to create blurred liquid spots on the surface. Splash on a little methylated spirit and allow to run in rivulets.

stencilling

Using stencils you can embellish items of furniture with painted patterns and motifs without any need to be a skilled artist. Stencils are versatile – they can be simple delicate flourishes or complex two-tone images; you can repeat them endlessly, mirror them, or create borders. The stately kitchen dresser in the picture opposite, dragged in tones of blue-grey, utilizes some of these qualities with its twin bowls of fruit reversed on each door, a border along the top which picks out fruit and foliage from the bowls, and simple stylized leaves forming corner flourishes and garlands. Such proliferation of pattern and texture needs no additional colour and the stencils have been rendered in a mottled charcoal that complements the colour of the dresser perfectly.

Above: A richly coloured chest-of-drawers, flanked by country-style chairs
in a kitchen setting, is adorned with colourful, busy stencils, repeated on
drawer fronts, knobs and chair slats to create a unified feel.

MATERIALS

Stencilling

CLEAR ACRYLIC FILM
FELT-TIPPED PEN
SCALPEL OR SHARP CRAFT KNIFE
CUTTING BOARD
SPRAY-ON ADHESIVE
NEWSPAPER
MASKING TAPE
STENCIL BRUSH
EMULSION OR SPRAY PAINT
CARD (FOR MASKING)

Although there are many pre-cut stencil kits on the market, designing and making your own is far more rewarding, and enables you to create unique patterns for your furniture. As a start, however, the stencil designs for the dresser are given on page 89, for you to trace, enlarge, reduce or otherwise adapt for this project. Inspiration for originating your own stencils can come from numerous sources – magazines, books, holiday snapshots, packaging, fabrics, wallpaper books and so on – and once you understand the basics of designing and cutting these versatile templates, you will find this technique the more exciting.

Simple designs, such as the stylized leaves, are just shaped holes cut in the stencil film; more complicated designs, such as the border and bowl of fruit, consist of a series of shapes which must be linked or 'bridged' to hold the stencil together in one piece. Stencils are conventionally cut from oiled manila card, but clear acrylic film is easier to use because it allows you to see through the stencil as a guide to positioning.

You can colour the stencil with spray paint, sold in automobile and do-it-yourself shops, or by stippling on emulsion with a stubby-bristled stencil brush – the latter option gives you more choice of colours, but both methods are quick and easy to apply.

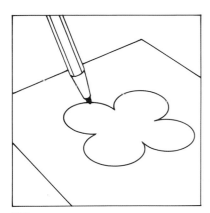

1 Place the stencil film over your chosen design and trace around it with a felt-tipped pen. For clarity, shade in the areas you are going to cut out.

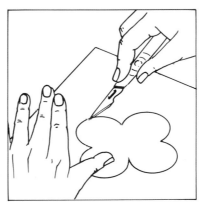

2 Place the film on a cutting board and cut around the drawn outlines carefully using a sharp craft knife or scalpel, taking care not to slice towards your fingers. If you accidentally slice through one of the delicate 'bridges', say in the border design, simply stick it back together with adhesive tape.

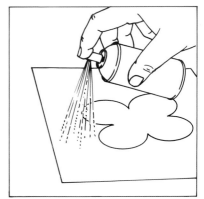

3 The stencil must be stuck flat to the surface you are decorating so that no paint bleeds underneath and blurs the edges of the design. Turn the cut stencil face down on a sheet of newspaper and spray the back with a thin even coat of low-tack adhesive, which will not harm the surface.

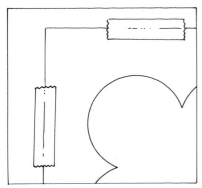

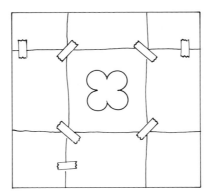

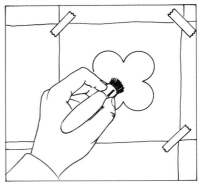

4 If you do not want to use spray-on adhesive you can simply stick the stencil in position with masking tape at the edges, although you will have to press the film firmly against the surface when applying the paint.

5 With the stencil secured, mask off around it with paper and masking tape to protect the adjoining areas.

6 You can apply the paint to the stencil using a stencilling brush, which gives a coarser texture than spray paint. Dip the bristles into the paint, then dab off the excess on to a piece of card. Apply the paint to the stencil with a rapid stippling action, making sure that it covers the edges of the design or it will appear incomplete.

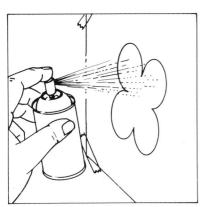

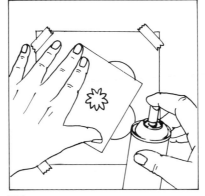

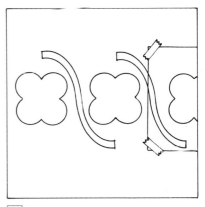

7 For a softer effect, use spray paint. Hold the can about 15cm (6in) away from the surface and at a slight angle, moving it closer for more delicate details of the design. Press the nozzle gently to produce a fine mist and move the can slightly from side to side to distribute the paint.

8 If you are applying two or more colours to the stencil, use a piece of card as a guard to prevent colours from reaching certain parts of the design. For very small details, cut a hole in the guard and place the hole over the feature to direct the spray accurately without touching other parts.

9 When applying a border design, work out in advance how the pattern fits across the furniture and centralize it if necessary, allowing the stencil to break off neatly at each end. Colour the first section, then move the stencil along, align it and colour the second, ensuring that the right-hand side of the design merges perfectly with the left-hand side.

combing

A new fitted kitchen can be expensive, but if you are tired of your old units, yet can't afford to buy new ones, why not simply give your old units a bright new look? Criss-cross combed patterns formed in coloured glaze can create a coarse fabric-like appearance, which both enhances and softens the harsh lines of a modern kitchen base unit like the one in the picture opposite. Combing is an effect which is easy to apply, so long as you work quickly and positively. A rubber-toothed triangular comb is drawn through the wet glaze to create a series of lines through which the base colour is visible; when drawn across at right-angles the effect resembles a coarsely woven hessian. You can create numerous different combed designs by drawing the comb through the glaze in wavy, diagonal or random motions, while different combinations of colours also produce interesting effects.

Above: Evocative of ethnic African colours, this umbrella stand is decorated
with an alternating series of wavy and angular lines combed in a thick
orangy glaze over a dark terracotta basecoat.

Combed kitchen unit
KITCHEN BASE UNIT
COARSE- MEDIUM- AND FINE-
GRADE ABRASIVE PAPER
WHITE SEMI-GLOSS PAINT
(BASECOAT)
PAINTBRUSH, PAD OR ROLLER
(FOR BASECOAT)
OIL-BASED GLOSS PAINT
WHITE SPIRIT
PAINTBRUSH (FOR GLAZE)
RUBBER COMB
CLEAR GLOSS OR SEMI-GLOSS
POLYURETHANE VARNISH

Before combing, the surface of the kitchen unit must be abraded with coarse-, medium- and then fine-grade abrasive paper to key it to accept the basecoat. If the unit is clad with plastic laminate, you should also apply a coat of primer before the basecoat, as the shiny surface would otherwise give a poor bond.

Here a pure white semi-gloss was used as the basecoat to accentuate the blue combing colour. Traditionally, combing uses transparent oil glazes coloured with artist's oil paints because the mixture offers an attractive translucency and slow drying, making for more controlled manipulation. However, in practice not many people can allow their kitchen to be out of commission for the three or four days it would take to dry. An easier method is to use ordinary oil-based gloss paint thinned with white spirit, which dries much more rapidly.

Paint on the glaze in a self-contained section of the unit, such as a complete door, so that you can finish the combing while the glaze is still wet. The rubber comb is triangular so that you can run three clean lines before you have to wipe off the excess glaze, making the job quicker. When you have use the three sides, dip each in turn into a container of white spirit and then wipe on to a rag. Continue combing, using the three sides of the comb again, and so on to complete the pattern. Comb the edges of the doors and drawers carefully, to avoid the teeth flicking on to the face and defacing the previous finish.

1 Remove the drawers, take the doors off their hinges, and then prepare them to accept the basecoat of paint. Apply the basecoat of semi-gloss paint with a brush, pad or roller and allow to dry, overcoating if necessary to cover a dark finish.

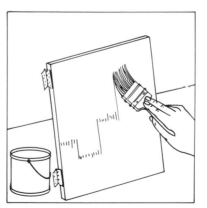

2 Paint the glaze of oil-based gloss paint thinned with white spirit on to a self-contained section of the unit, such as a drawer front or door. The layer of the glaze should be fairly thin but even in coverage.

3 Immediately, take the comb and draw it firmly across the glaze, starting at the left-hand side and working to the right (vice versa if you are left-handed). Keep the comb as straight as possible as you move it, so that the series of lines does not waver too much.

Once the combing is complete and the glaze dry, apply two or three coats of clear polyurethane varnish in gloss or semi-gloss finish to protect the surface from the spills and knocks to which it is bound to be susceptible in the kitchen.

COMBED PATTERNS

The diagrams show the many and varied patterns which can be created by combing: zig-zag, cross-hatched, wavy and random.

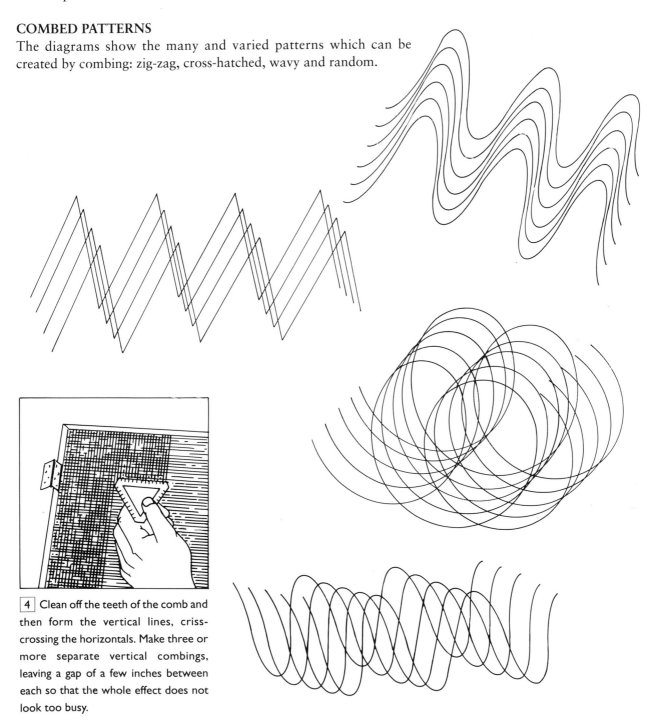

4 Clean off the teeth of the comb and then form the vertical lines, criss-crossing the horizontals. Make three or more separate vertical combings, leaving a gap of a few inches between each so that the whole effect does not look too busy.

lining

Simulate the look of a crisp cotton cloth draped over a slim but stately hall table, as shown in the photograph opposite, with emulsion-painted bands of grey on a white background and darker slate-grey legs protruding. Such a monochromatic scheme needs only the simplest of accessories, so that attention is drawn solely to the table, which becomes a handsome focal point. The stripes are formed by a small sponge paint roller, with its end cut squarely and a slim line cut a few millimetres away. Loaded with paint and drawn lightly across the white-painted tabletop and around the sides, the grey emulsion produces a mottled, slightly undulating appearance that resembles fabric.

Above: A more bizarre lined effect ideal for the playroom: a small bookshelf
is adorned with multi-coloured lines applied in one pass of a paperhanger's
brush plucked of some of its bristles (see 'tip box', page 79) and the
remaining clumps dipped into different coloured paints.

MATERIALS

Chequered hall table
RECTANGULAR HALL TABLE
PAINT STRIPPER
MEDIUM- AND FINE-GRADE
ABRASIVE PAPER
WHITE SPIRIT
WHITE AND BLACK MATT
EMULSION PAINT
PAINTBRUSH, PAD OR ROLLER
SCALPEL
ROLLER TRAY
MASKING TAPE
OIL-BASED BLACKBOARD PAINT
(OPTIONAL)
CLEAR MATT SPRAY-ON GLAZE

For this project, you will need to work out the spacing of the pale grey stripes running from front to back of the table, in order to determine the gaps between each and the way they fall in relation to the edge of the table. Also work out the position for the darker grey stripes running at right-angles, and allow for a single darker stripe running around the front of the tabletop.

Apply the paler stripes first, loading the roller only moderately with paint; the aim is for slightly patchy coverage. There is no need to hurry when rolling on the stripes, as long as you do not exert uneven pressure on the roller, which would cause darker, filled-in areas to be applied. If, after completing a stripe, you are not satisfied with the coverage, there is no reason why you cannot go over the same stripe again, but with lighter pressure and without reloading the roller.

Wait until the pale stripes are dry before applying the darker ones, at right-angles. Complete the table by painting the legs in a dark, streaky grey – try mixing oil-based blackboard paint with white emulsion for an interesting, slaty effect. Although oil- and water-based paints should not really be mixed, there is no reason why not for such a small, easily repainted feature.

As the completed table is covered only in emulsion, the surface will not be durable. However, you can add protection, also helping to seal the surface, with an aerosol-type clear glaze in matt finish.

1 Strip off any previous paint, varnish or polish from the table and then sand with medium- followed by fine-grade abrasive paper. Remove the knobs or handles – these can be painted in the same colour as the table legs for continuity. Wipe over the surface with white spirit then allow to dry.

2 Apply two or more coats of matt white emulsion to the tabletop for complete coverage, using a paintbrush, roller or pad.

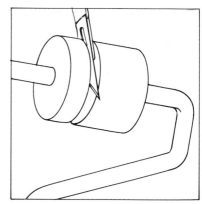

3 Cut the end off the roller, then mark a 50mm (2in) wide line 6–12mm (¼–½in) from the end and cut around the foam with a scalpel. Trim away the foam to leave a gap.

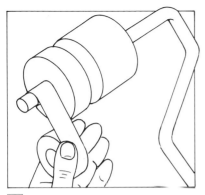

4 Wrap masking tape around the cut-off end of the roller so that the foam is held in place. Then wrap another strip around the narrower slot to stiffen the edges of the roller.

5 Mix up the pale grey paint by adding a small amount of black to the white and stirring thoroughly. Trickle in the black from a teaspoon so that you do not add too much. Make sure you have enough paint to complete the stripes, as mixing more of the identical shade will be difficult.

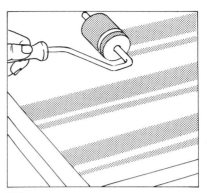

6 Load the cut-down roller with paint and apply the first band to the white tabletop in a slow, steady movement. Go over the band if necessary for greater coverage and then continue with subsequent bands.

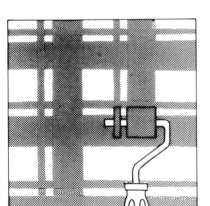

7 Mix up some darker grey paint and complete the bands at right-angles to the paler ones.

8 Paint the legs of the table with matt grey emulsion paint, or a streaky combination of oil-based blackboard paint and emulsion; the two different paints do not mix well, so the resultant coverage is an interesting grey streaked with white and black. Seal the surface of the table with clear matt spray-on glaze.

TIP

A paperhanger's brush, with chunks of bristles cut off, creates an excellent segmented brush for applying several colours of paint in one go, as on the playroom toy shelf on page 76. Wrap around the base of the sections of bristles with masking tape so that they do not separate.

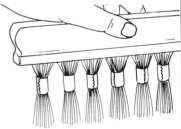

Paint the shelf unit in white emulsion and leave to dry. Dip the bristles of the trimmed brush into little pots of your chosen colours, diluted with white spirit to create a semi-transparent glaze. Apply to the shelf unit in bold stripes.

distressing

The worn faded appearance of old painted wood that evolves naturally with the passage of time has a mellow beauty that complements rustic-style schemes perfectly. The well-used appearance of the aged meatsafe in the picture opposite, for instance – now used as a novel but practical home for crusty bread and eggs in a beamed country kitchen – is nothing less than pure fabrication, brought about by clever use of paint and wax polish. The art of 'distressing', or artificial ageing, can be used to invest even bright new or poor-quality wooden furniture with a period charm or noble maturity, as demonstrated by the modern pine bedhead in the picture below, which has been infused with the romantic air of an eighteenth-century boudoir.

Above: White lacy pillows are offset by the delicate blue-green tones of this
artificially aged bedhead, which in reality is a modern pine type overlaid
with varnish, green then blue emulsion, and then partially abraded to reveal
the layers beneath. Beeswax provides the delicate sheen and protects the
faux finish from real ageing.

MATERIALS

Distressed cabinet
WOODEN CABINET
PAINT STRIPPER
WIRE WOOL
WHITE SPIRIT
MID-BROWN VARNISH
POWDER BLUE AND SAGE GREEN
SATIN-FINISH EMULSION PAINT
75MM (3IN) PAINTBRUSH
MEDIUM- AND FINE-GRADE
ABRASIVE PAPER
BEESWAX
RAGS
DARK TAN SHOE POLISH

Distressing can be carried out on both old and new wood, but both will need some preparation to accept the emulsion paint used to create the *faux* finish. On new wood, strip off any existing paint or varnish using a proprietary liquid, gel or paste stripper. Do not worry unduly if patches of previous finish are stubborn to come off – say in moulded parts – because this can contribute to the 'ageing' effect that you are trying to achieve. With old wood, you may have to remove previous coats of wax polish by rubbing gently with white spirit and wire wool, then sanding, washing with detergent and rinsing.

The green colour of the meatsafe is one that is fairly traditional in English and Scandinavian artisan furniture, and on many examples a blue colouring shows through. The opposite scheme – blue on green – has been adopted for the bedhead, which evokes the softer, more elegant style of eighteenth-century French furniture. Satin-finish emulsion has been used here because the subtle sheen it produces enhances the effect.

When distressing new or very light-coloured wood which you have varnished to darken the tone (see below), avoid removing the varnish layer or the lighter tone will mar the effect. Boot polish rubbed on to the paint and spread out with a rag will further enhance the aged effect, and a final coat of beeswax gives a subtle sheen and helps to protect the finish.

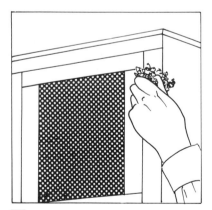

1 Strip off previous paint or varnish finishes with a proprietary stripper and remove any build-up of wax by rubbing with wire wool soaked in white spirit. Wipe over with white spirit and leave to dry. On new pine or other light-coloured wood, apply a coat of mid-brown varnish to darken the tone.

2 Apply the first colour of satin emulsion paint liberally using a 75mm (3in) paintbrush, and allow to dry thoroughly before proceeding with the second colour. Always brush the paint along the direction of the wood grain, finishing with light brushstrokes.

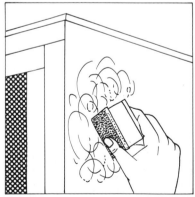

3 Once the topcoat of paint has dried, start to abrade areas carefully, using medium-grade abrasive paper. Start off with it wrapped around a wooden block and use light pressure so as to dull areas of the sheen without penetrating the top layer of paint.

4 Remove the abrasive paper from the block and fold it so that it has a narrow, rounded edge. Use it in this manner to remove streaks of paint across the surface, allowing the original wood colour – or the varnished layer – to be revealed.

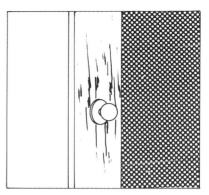

5 Concentrate your rubbing at the edges of the cabinet and at the corners, as these are the areas that would naturally receive most wear. Other areas to pay particular attention to are around door handles and knobs, and edges where generations of fingers would erode a paint finish.

6 Minor defects, such as gouges, dents and splits, will actually help to enhance the aged look of the furniture. Wipe them over with dark tan shoe polish applied with a rag to darken them, especially on new wood.

7 Remember not to overdo the ageing, or the result will be merely scruffy rather than mature. When you are satisfied with the overall appearance of the cabinet, treat the entire item with a coat of beeswax applied with a cloth and buffed to a subtle sheen.

8 Moulded or carved areas deserve special attention, as it is essential not to remove all the paint from these features by too rigorous abrading. Aim for a patchy effect, where raised parts are abraded to bare wood and crevices contain thicker deposits of the original paint colour.

It is always interesting to add some special decorative touches to your painted furniture, perhaps to highlight particular features, and then to protect it from harm with a clear finish that does not conceal your handiwork.

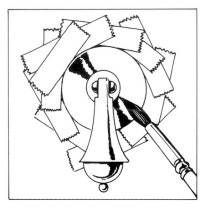

If you do not trust your freehand, mask off the area around the decorative feature, and then apply the gold or silver enamel paint liberally by brush, working it into any details.

EMBELLISHMENTS

You can enhance the beauty of your painted furniture by ornamenting it with highlights of gold or silver, or glittering motifs, and even embellish plain painted surfaces with printed paper motifs applied by the technique of découpage.

Easy gilding

Traditional gilding with metal leaf or powder, although undoubtedly a beautiful means of adding adornment to wooden items, is a prohibitively costly and highly skilled technique. But there is a far easier and quicker way to add sparkling golden touches to components of your furniture, using cheap modelmaker's enamel paints.

The success of these 'gilded' highlights depends on moderation and the careful selection of existing ornamentation on the furniture to be gilded – perhaps a small carved flourish on a plain background, an ornate finial (such as the balled tops of the combed umbrella stand on page 72) or a fretwork insert (as on the freehand painted corner cabinet on page 57). Even a knob or handle coloured gold or silver (such as those on the chequered grey-and-white hall table on page 77) would add a richness that enhances the overall appearance of the finished piece.

Sparkling texture

Add glinting features to plain areas of painted wood by sticking fine, coloured Christmas glitter to the surface and then sealing with varnish or spray-on glaze. Paint or stencil motifs, such as stars, moons or stylized floral designs, on to the furniture, using an all-purpose adhesive, and then sprinkle on the glitter. When the adhesive is dry, blow off the surplus glitter to leave the motif clearly defined.

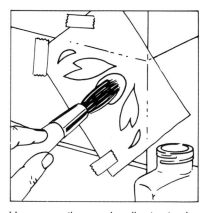

Use a stencil to apply adhesive in the shape of your chosen motif and then sprinkle on the glitter. Blow off the surplus to reveal the motif.

Here the golds and deep blues of mirrors, candlesticks and walls are combined in an interesting sponged treatment for cupboard doors.

1 Cut out an image from a magazine, book or other source, using a sharp scalpel knife.

Pasted paper cut-outs

Découpage, the long-established technique of sticking paper cut-outs on to a flat surface, colouring and then sealing them, is an ideal way to decorate your painted furniture with beautiful motifs or quirky designs. You can cut out images from magazines or books, or photocopy motifs from books on historical ornament and use the copies as cut-outs.

The cut-out, coated both sides with a liquid solution of wallpaper paste and water, is brushed on to the painted surface, to which it sticks perfectly flat. You can then use diluted emulsion, gouache, artist's oils or acrylics to colour black and white images.

Once decorated, successive applications of clear varnish will protect the cut-outs, prevent them from lifting and, if you apply several coats, give an excellent depth of finish.

2 Coat the cut-out on both sides with a wallpaper-paste solution. Then position it on the furniture and brush the cut-out flat.

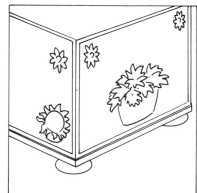

3 Apply successive coats of polyurethane varnish to seal and protect the cut-out.

4 Photocopied images can be used in découpage and coloured with diluted emulsion. Colour photocopies can also be used to interesting effect.

VARNISHING

Varnish provides timber with a protective film, without concealing its grain or the decorative paint effect you have applied, or altering its colour. There are coloured varnishes, however, which can be used to tint the wood or paint finish.

Varnish consists of a resin, which gives a hard finish, carried in a drying oil or spirit, with pigments added for coloured types. Polyurethane varnishes offer the most durable finish and are available in matt, gloss or satin (semi-gloss) finishes. Use matt for painted furniture with a non-shiny finish; gloss for the most-used items and surfaces such as tabletops and chair seats, which will receive knocks and spills; and satin for other examples of moderate wear. Several coats of varnish can be applied to produce a superior depth of finish.

Apply varnish on a dry day in a warm, dust-free, ventilated room. Stand the furniture on improvized blocks so that you can treat all parts and leave to dry for at least 24 hours.

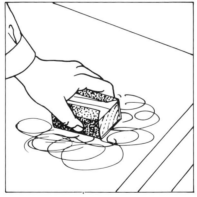

1 Make sure the furniture to be varnished is free from grease, even fingermarks, by wiping over with white spirit. Apply the initial coat of varnish with a clean wad of lint-free cloth, rubbing the liquid along the wood grain. If this is not visible, work in one direction only for smoothest coverage.

2 When the first coat of varnish has dried – most surfaces can be recoated after about 12 hours – sand down lightly with fine-grade abrasive paper and then dust off.

3 Apply the subsequent coats of varnish with a well-loaded brush, so that the liquid flows on to the surface. Brush it out lightly, avoiding brushmarks, bubbles and runs. Sand when the varnish has dried, and then repeat two or three times more. Matt varnish does not require sanding between coats.

Polishing

Even a varnished finish will benefit from polishing to enhance the lustre. Rub on a wax polish with a clean lint-free cloth, using a series of circular motions and working across the surface. Use a second cloth to buff up the wax to a sheen. On large areas you can use a padded buffing attachment to an electric drill.

Electric drill complete with buffing attachment.

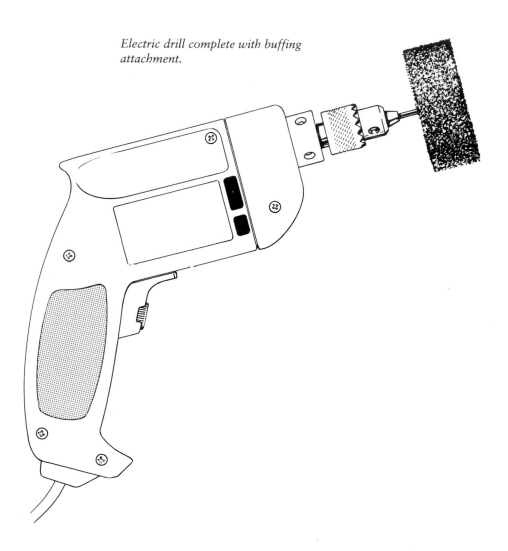

the templates

Sponge-stencilled starfish, shells and seahorses create a bright nautical effect in the bathroom illustrated on page 49. The templates for these stencils are overleaf.

The elegant kitchen dresser on page 69 is decorated with stencilled fruit and foliage. Use the templates on page 91 to achieve this effect.

INDEX

Page numbers in *italic* refer to illustrations